Harley-Davidson and Philosophy

Popular Culture and Philosophy™
Series Editor: William Irwin

Popular Culture and Philosophy™

Harley-Davidson and Philosophy

Full-Throttle Aristotle

Edited by

BERNARD E. ROLLIN, CAROLYN M. GRAY,
KERRI MOMMER, and CYNTHIA PINEO

OPEN COURT
Chicago and La Salle, Illinois

Volume 18 in the series, Popular Culture and Philosophy™

**To order books from Open Court, call 1-800-815-2280, or visit
www.opencourtbooks.com.**

Open Court Publishing Company is a division of Carus Publishing
Company.

Library of Congress Cataloging-in-Publication Data

Harley-Davidson and philosophy : full-throttle Aristotle / edited by
Bernard E. Rollin . . . [et al.].
    p. cm. — (Popular culture and philosophy ; v. 18)
    Includes bibliographical references and index.
    ISBN-13: 978-0-8126-9595-3 (trade pbk. : alk. paper)
    ISBN-10: 0-8126-9595-X (trade pbk. : alk. paper)
    1. Motorcycling--Philosophy. 2. Harley-Davidson Incorporated.
I. Rollin, Bernard E. II. Series.
GV1059.5.H37 2006
629.2'275—dc22
                                          2005031878

To Iron Mike, my riding partner, dialogue partner and best bro since he was born. To Linda, the love of my life for forty-two years. Thank you both for assuring I keep the rubber to the road and thanks for a great ride.

    —B.E.R.

To my wonderful parents, Mary and Willie Madia, now you guys can answer that question "Who's Harley-Davidson?" To my brother Billy Madia, his wife Chris and daughter Gillian, I just have to say Long Live Eric Waxman! *To my Hoosier in-laws, Brenda and Gary Gray, thanks for teaching me the two most important words in the English language . . . GO PACERS! And to my husband David Gray, I thank God I get to go on life's journey with you.*

    —C.M.G.

To Arlo, my very favorite bike buddy and Yu-Gi-Oh expert extraordinaire, *and David, my beloved life partner and the best philosopher in our family—thank you for all your support both on and off the road. To Rol and Eva, I'll always remember our fantastic trip of summer 2005.*

    —K.M.

To Mike, Bob, Linda, Richard, and Angie. Thanks for all the adventures on the road, and for believing in this book.

    —C.P.

Contents

Third Leg: 300 Miles

Last Leg: 400 Miles

Foreword

R.K. STRATMAN

When asked to write a foreward for a book about philosophy, I wondered what I might have to say. I am not a philosopher. I am just a man who loves what he does. I am a father of seven, a grandfather of twelve, and a great-grandfather of two. I am not an MBA, but I am a graduate of life, a self-made man, and a born salesman. I am not a suit; I am an ex-racer, a motorcycle rider and a lover of the open road. After reading several of the essays I felt intimidated. For the last thirty-six years my family and I have printed, merchandised, and sold Harley-Davidson t-shirts at the races, HD dealerships, rallies, and events. What can I offer about the philosophy of Harley-Davidson?

As a young teen, I became determined to have a motorcycle. My first ride was in the parking lot of my high school on a friend's bike. As soon as I felt the wind on my face I knew I had to have one. When I finally earned enough money for a motorcycle, I entered my first race. At the time I had a growing family of four, and soon my son started to race as well. We turned it into a family affair, my wife and girls selling iron-on patches and decals at the races to support our racing habits. That weekend venture has now grown to a company of two-hundred-plus employees, operating out of three buildings in two cities, and is still fully owned and operated by family. My daughter, Tammy, always said we were in the t-shirt business; I always felt my job was in the Harley business.

In 1978 I started a motorcycle collection consisting of the firsts and lasts of engine models, and later added the infamous Buffalo Bike. My teenage obsession of fun and freedom has become a lifelong adventure. Whether Harleys become a part of your profession or just a weekend escape, the ride consumes you. Perhaps the allure is the freedom of the open road, or the escape from conformity. Maybe it is the immediate bond and brotherhood shared with fellow riders. It could be the pride and reliability in the American-made machine. Whatever it is, over the years, the biker's image has been altered into a stereotype and a pop-culture phenomenon. The only way to know the difference is to ride. It is not an attraction that can be put into words. The real rider in the "biker bar" knows "why."

So, what can I offer about the philosophy of Harley-Davidson? All that comes to mind is a phrase that has sold in our t-shirt line for over twenty years. "IF I have to Explain, you wouldn't Understand."

R.K. Stratman on his Buffalo Bike.

Mile Zero

A small change at the beginning produces many great changes at a distance, just as a tiny shift in a boat's rudder causes a huge shift of the prow.

—ARISTOTLE (*On the Movement of Animals*, 701b, 25–28)

Author Bernard E. Rollin with his 1986 Harley-Davidson low-rider (FXRS).

Introduction:
When Your Life Revolves around Harleys

BERNARD E. ROLLIN

Some years ago, my son and I took a two-week motorcycle trip to Wyoming and Montana and stopped at Yellowstone. Before we left the park we, in good tourist fashion, went to watch Old Faithful erupt. We just missed it, but were assured it would go again in twenty-five minutes or so. As the twenty-five minutes became closer to an hour, we struck up a conversation with an outlaw biker from L.A. We had a marvelous conversation; he was both a well-informed and a witty conversationalist. But a shadow hung over the discussion, rooted in my fear that he would ask me what I was thinking of as "the Dreaded Question," namely, "What do you do for a living?" Had Old Faithful been truer to its name, I might have avoided the Dreaded Question; but it was not.

About five minutes prior to eruption, he did indeed turn to me and asked, "Say, what do you do for a living?" I briefly contemplated a variety of plausible falsehoods I could fake—"I am a welder . . . a cowboy . . . a construction worker." But I was raised to tell the truth, and anyway figured his response to the truth would probably make for a good story. Steeling myself, I squeaked, "Actually, I'm a philosophy professor." At this point, he leaped off his bike, embraced me enthusiastically and intoned, "Gee that's great! You have a steady job so you can keep the bike running!"

I have told that story many times since then, much to the amusement of my audiences. But the story contains a number of points directly relevant to the subject matter of this book, the Harley-Davidson way of life, that are worth discussing.

In the first place, the easy camaraderie that our conversation evidenced is typical of what occurs when Harley riders of all backgrounds meet under any circumstance. There is an instant bonding that can be found among fraternity brothers, Shriners, and former New Yorkers. Some of it is, of course, very simply the brotherhood of people evidenced in those who share a common interest. But there is something extra among Harley Riders that is elusive to characterize, but exists nonetheless. It is not only a sense of shared pursuit, but also a kind of quiet elitism stemming from absolute certainty that one is privy to something that most people will neither experience nor understand. I hope the essays in this book will help explain this *je ne sais quoi*.

Second, the story evidences the fact that the biker automatically assumed that everything—even one's profession—revolves around and is ancillary to one's time on the motorcycle. Whether the biker is a professor, an outlaw, a surgeon, a lawyer, or a plumber, the motorcycle is never far from the center of one's consciousness. On one occasion, I went for a ride with a friend who was not an experienced rider; she promptly crashed the motorcycle on a rural road, cracking three ribs and breaking her clavicle. Fortunately, we were not far from Laramie, Wyoming, and what is arguably the nicest hospital either of us had ever been in. Within thirty minutes we were in the emergency room, and a trauma surgeon was examining her. After finishing his examination and telling me the damage, he looked me in the eye and said, "God damn you and your friend! If it weren't for the two of you I would be out riding my Harley on this fine summer day." That anecdote tells it all.

In this book, we have attempted to collect a variety of philosophical reflections on the unique phenomenon of Harleys and their riders. If some of our readers choose to explore riding a Harley further, my time will have been well spent.

THE RIDE

The now corresponds to the traveling thing, just as time corresponds to motion. For the traveling thing gives us knowledge of the before and after in motion, and the now is what makes the before and after countable.

—ARISTOTLE *(Physics,* Book IV, Chapter 11, 23–24)

FIRST LEG:
100 Miles

We also come to know motion because of the thing in motion, and travel because of the thing traveling. In a way, then, the now is always the same, and in a way it is not. For the same is true of the thing traveling.

—ARISTOTLE (*Physics*, Book IV, Chapter 11, 29–33)

1

Zen and the Art of Harley Riding

GRAHAM PRIEST

Transcend discrimination of opposites, discover total reality, and achieve detachment. This is complete freedom.

Dōgen (*Shobogenzo*, Chapter 3)

Pirsig's Paradoxical Book

Motorcycles and Zen don't seem very natural bedfellows. When we think of Zen, we normally think of a monk seated peacefully in meditation in the tranquility of a temple or a garden. If there's any noise at all, it's the ringing of a temple bell or the chirping of birds or cicadas. By contrast, motor bikes are noisy, exciting, dangerous—almost the exact opposite. To try to put the two things together would seem to be paradoxical in the extreme.

So when Robert Pirsig decided to face this paradox, putting the two things together in what was to become the classic *Zen and the Art of Motorcycle Maintenance* (first published in 1974), this was an act of great daring.

I read the book for the first time in 1976. At that time, I had been riding a motorcycle for about six years—and doing my own maintenance (with the help of friends who knew more than I did), since I couldn't afford to pay anybody else to do it. I had been teaching philosophy at a university in Scotland for a couple of years; but I knew virtually nothing about Zen, except what one can learn from the back of cereal boxes. I bought the book to read on the plane that was taking me to Australia, where I was moving to a new job (and where I have lived ever since). I read the book on the twenty-five-hour journey, also wondering what the new life would have in store for me.

The book was a good yarn, and I enjoyed Pirsig's obvious knowledge about bikes—whether or not his bike was a Harley. (The narrator in the book never, in fact, says what his bike is; but I assume that it probably was a Harley since the make dominated the American market at the time.) But the book didn't seem to me to have much to do with Zen. I took Pirsig at his word when he said, in a note at the beginning of the book, that what goes on between its covers "should in no way be associated with that great body of factual information relating to orthodox Zen Buddhist practice."

The second time I read the book was twenty-eight years later. I was still riding a motorcycle (a Harley, which I could now afford), but not doing my own maintenance any more. By that time I had been teaching philosophy for thirty years and, moreover, knew a lot more about Zen. Indeed, I was again on a plane, returning from a conference in Australia to Kyoto where I was spending some months studying—amongst other things— Zen. Again, I read the book in one sitting.

And this time it seemed to me that Pirsig's disclaimer about Zen was, deliberately or otherwise, far too modest.

Ultimate Reality and the Conceptual Grid

To explain why, I must say a little bit about Zen. A fundamental idea of Zen (and a number of other branches of Buddhism) is that there is an *ultimate reality* of a certain kind. It goes by various names, such as "Buddha nature," "ultimate mind," or "emptiness." We are not normally aware of it. What we are aware of is what is produced when we impose our own conceptual grid on this reality, often called *conventional reality* in the Buddhist tradition.

Think of it like this. A motorcycle is a single functioning unit; but we can cut it up intellectually by applying certain concepts to it. *This is the carburetor. This is the fuel tank. The fuel flows from the tank through the carburetor into the combustion chamber.* But we can cut it up in quite different ways with different concepts. *These are the rubber bits. These are the chrome bits. The rubber bits are softer than the chrome bits.* But the bike itself is just what it is, however we choose to conceptualize it.

So it is with ultimate reality. We can conceptualize it in many ways. In doing so, we arrive at reality of a conventional kind. (Conventional in that a different set of concepts could have cut the reality up in different ways.) Ultimate reality itself, however, is just what it is, independent of any conceptual grid we choose to apply to it. And how is that? Well, you can't say. To say it is like *this*, or like *that*, is to apply a conceptual grid to it, not to say what it is like in itself. In ultimate reality, there are no distinctions, no *thises* rather than *thats*. Such distinctions disappear. There is just a simple "suchness."

The *Genjokoan* Experience and Riding

One of the most fundamental aims of Zen Buddhism is to get people to experience this suchness, to strip back the conceptual grids, and be directly aware of ultimate reality. The great Japanese Zen theorist, Dōgen, called this experience *genjokoan*.

In the *genjokoan* experience, all distinctions vanish. Perhaps the most important distinction is that between the person doing the thinking and the thing that they are thinking about. This distinction vanishes too. There is no distinct subject, no distinct object. Subject and object are one.

This may all sound very strange. What on earth is it like?

A standard way of obtaining the *genjokoan* experience is by kneeling meditation, *zazen*. Not that one can just expect to kneel down and experience *genjokoan*. Mental focus of a very disciplined kind is required, and this may take years of practice. You have to work hard at it until, paradoxically, it just comes naturally. (The importance of naturalness is one of the imports from Taoism into Zen.)

It may well be that *zazen* is a particularly important or robust way of coming to experience *genjokoan*. But even Zen theorists don't think it's the only way. It can be acquired through any practice of mental concentration, which, when carried out often enough, comes naturally. This can be achieved though a martial art, the tea ceremony, flower arrangement, or in any number of other ways.

I think that most bike riders have experienced *genjokoan*, at least in some form. When you start to learn to drive a bike, it's very hard. It requires intense concentration. *First pull the clutch in with your left hand. Then kick the gear lever up with your left foot. Then let the clutch out. While you are doing this, keep your eyes on the road. Watch for stupid car drivers pulling out of side roads who don't see anything smaller than a car.* . . . But one of the miracles of learning to drive is that eventually this becomes entirely natural. You don't have to think about it at all any more. You just do it.

And when it reaches this stage, driving can be a vehicle for the *genjokoan* experience. This happens most, I think, on long trips on the open road. After a while one just forgets that one is driving. One ceases to think about that. One ceases to think about anything, in fact. There is just the road, the elements, the driving. There is not even a you that is doing the driving. You *are* the driving—and the road, and the elements. Maybe this is not the purest form of *genjokoan*. It is certainly not the most robust. It has a tendency to disappear very fast when, for example, an oncoming truck thunders past you, hogging too much of your side of the road—unless you have nerves that are made of harder steel than mine. But it is a *genjokoan* experience, nonetheless.

It is possible to get the experience just as much when you drive a car, as well. But there is something special about a bike. You can feel one with a bike in a way in which it is difficult to feel one with a car. On a bike you move with it, lean with it. You are one with it. You also experience the elements directly: the wind, the rain. You are one with the elements. None of this is true of a car. In a car, you are hermetically sealed. There is a sense in which you always feel like a passenger, even if you are driving.

I have also found Harleys more conducive to the experience than other bikes. I have driven lots of bikes over the years, BSAs, Yamahas, BMWs. It's only in the last seven years that I have driven a Harley. But I have had the experience more on this bike than any other. Maybe it's because I am getting older, or know better what to look for. But there is something distinctive about riding a Harley. The sitting position is relaxed. You are not leaned forward with your chest over your knees. The engine does not whine. Indeed, because the engine is very low-revving, it never feels as though you are going fast, even if you are. And as the bike drops into top gear, you get that characteristic *thug, thug, thug*—a hypnotic rhythm that must resonate with some fundamental frequency in the human brain.

Genjokoan and Thought

Anyway, oddly enough Pirsig says little about this—though the discussion of Quality towards the very end of the book starts to come close to the topic of ultimate reality. Maybe it's too easy. As the title of the book indicates, what he talks about a lot more than driving a bike is maintaining it. This might seem odd. Not many bikers have experienced the *genjokoan* experience when working on their bikes. For a start, repairing a bike would seem to involve a lot of the conceptual thinking which *genjokoan* is meant to strip off. *The bike is not idling evenly. Maybe one of the plugs needs to be cleaned or replaced. I'd better pull them out and have a look.* Moreover, unless you are a mechanic and spend much of your time engaged in this sort of activity, it is unlikely that such thought processes will become entirely unreflective.

But things are not that simple.

The *genjokoan* experience can be had in many activities—maybe all of them if you have achieved the highest stage of enlightenment (namely, permanent *genjokoan*). Some of these must be conceptual. After all, Zen masters who achieved such enlightenment still gave highly intellectual lectures on the nature of Zen, such as Dōgen and the lectures recorded in his mammoth *Shobogenzo*. Isn't there a paradox in the fact that Zen masters, for whom cutting through the concealment generated by concepts—and thus by language—is so important, often produce highly technical tracts on the philosophy of Zen? Let's come back to this later.

While hardly wishing to compare myself with Dōgen, I can vouch that doing philosophy and other activities of a highly conceptual kind is not incompatible with *genjokoan*. I have sometimes sat down and started to think about a philosophical or a mathematical problem. The next thing I know, I look at the clock and an hour has elapsed. The intense concentration had produced a state in which there was no me thinking about something; nor was there a something for me to think about. There was just the thinking; just like, when driving a bike, there can be just the driving.

The core of the *genjokoan* experience is precisely this transcendence of the subject-object distinction. There is no you. There is no it. There is just a suchness. But no one said that this suchness must be bland and amorphous. It can be structured— by the dappled patches of light on the grass—by the features of the road when you drive—or by the features of an abstract problem. After all, Zen monks are often given problems of this kind on which to meditate: koans. (A koan is a conceptual puzzle that the monk is given to solve, such as the well-known "What is the sound of one hand clapping?" The word *koan*, incidentally, has many meanings; whether it means the same in the context as *genjokoan* is debatable.)

Zen and the Art of Motorcycle Maintenance

Now come back to motorcycle maintenance. This comes in many forms, all the way from cleaning the bike to remove the crud which will produce corrosion, to taking the engine apart and doing the big-ends. All bikers enjoy riding their bikes. But most (including, I must admit, myself) don't enjoy such maintenance. These are chores that you have to do to keep the bike up and running—or in an extreme case, to get it up and running. Time spent doing this is time you can't spend riding. So in this context, unlike when you are riding it, you tend to see the bike as an object, an imposition, something alien that requires you to dirty your hands and skin your knuckles.

The whole point of Pirsig's discussion of motorcycle maintenance is that this is a mistake. In motorcycle maintenance, one should feel one with the bike just as much as when one is riding it. Don't rush it; don't wish it to be over; don't think about all the other things you could be doing. Just focus on the job at hand and become one with what you are doing.

He's right about this. As he points out, in effect, you will find what you are doing more fulfilling if you think of it as an end in itself, not as an annoying means to something else that you really want to be doing. In other words, you will not feel alienated from what is going on. You will also do a better job. If you have 100 percent focus, you will not make stupid mistakes (which is not to say that you will not make mistakes).

But there are other reasons which he doesn't mention. Being what you are doing, in this way, is a form of *genjokoan*, of experiencing ultimate reality. That may sound pretty weird. Washing your bike is ultimate realty? Yes: ultimate reality is the reality of the here and now. There is no other to be experienced. You will do other things at other times. But when you do them, they, too, should be done in the same way. As the Zen saying goes: When you sit, sit; when you stand, stand; whatever you do, don't wobble.

And precisely because the experience is one of *genjokoan*, it has the effects that Pirsig points to. In all Buddhism, *genjokoan* is not an end in itself. Perhaps the most fundamental idea in Buddhism is that all of us in life are subject to unhappiness and suffering. We suffer, moreover, because of our ignorance: we understand the world wrong. When we see the world aright, the suffering and ill-being that trouble all things disappear. *Genjokoan* leads to well-being.

Buddhism and Compassion

We touch here on the ethical side of Buddhism—at least of Mahayana Buddhism, of which Zen is one kind. Buddhism is a compassionate religion. It cares about the well-being of all things. Ultimate reality is such that there is no distinction between things. You and I are not separate beings. If you think of yourself and myself as different and independent beings, this is just a result of imposing a certain conceptual grid on reality. In the end, this is simply a conceptual construction, and answers to nothing that is really there. In reality, there is no distinction between you and me. It follows that your well-being and my well-being cannot be distinguished.

And the well-being of the bike too. The distinction between yourself and myself has exactly the same status as that between my bike and myself. The distinctions between all things—you, me, the bike, everything else—answer to nothing in ultimate reality. Care of oneself, of others, of all things, all amount to the same thing—much as conceptual thinking may disguise this fact, or even make it appear absurdly false. (There is a certain irony in Pirsig's book on this point. The narrator is not at one with all things. He is not even at one with himself. Much of the book concerns the struggle between the narrator and a previous self, Phaedrus, who still lives within him.)

Ultimate and Conventional Reality

We started with an apparent paradox between Zen and motor-cycles. This turns out not to have been very deep. But the ruminations just past seem to have parlayed this into a much more profound paradox. Ultimate reality is, I said, independent of conceptualization; it is what remains when conceptualization is removed. I have also claimed that ultimate reality can be structured in a certain way, and that this structuring can be conceptual. How can both of these things be true? It's precisely the conceptual structuring that defines conventional reality and distinguishes it from ultimate reality. Ultimate reality and conventional reality would seem to be as fundamentally different as any two things could be.

But wait. Again this is too easy. In ultimate reality all distinctions, all dualities, disappear. There are no distinctions, not even the one between ultimate and conventional reality. Ultimate reality and conventional reality are one. The conceptualized must be identical with the unconceptualized!

The thought is a venerable one in Buddhism, and certainly predates Zen. But it is captured nicely in the Zen saying: Before I studied Zen, mountains were mountains and water was water. After I studied Zen for some time, mountains were no longer mountains, and water was no longer water. But now that I have studied Zen longer, I see that mountains are just mountains, and water is just water.

And for that matter, motorcycles are motorcycles. Though maybe not in the sense that you may think they are.

2
Christ in a Sidecar: An Ontology of Suicide Machines

RANDALL E. AUXIER

The title caught your attention. Was it the borrowed bit of Springsteen lyric coupled with that odd word in the subtitle, or the danger of taking a messianic name in vain? I do hope that such in-vanity is venal compared to the scarletude of the mortal sins that follow, but whatever may be the divine judgment, *voila*, you turned right to this chapter, so you're no better off than the other sinners. I know you're eager to hit the road and see who's in the sidecar, but you'll have to cool your twin-cams until the next chapter. Right now our trusty steed is up on blocks in the living room, so be patient. We have work to do first, but you won't be disappointed.

Workin' on a Hog?

We need some tools, and tools are not very exciting. Here's something boring to consider: Philosophical discussions really need to begin with an explicit "ontology," that is, an explicit specification of what entities, processes, and modes of existence will be under discussion. Not only does good ontology inhibit needless verbal disputes later, but it also forces us into a reflective frame of mind, a frame of mind in which we ask ourselves what Martin Heidegger called "the Question."[1]

---

[1] Many trees have given their lives in service of discussing the Question of Being, but the first trees to offer themselves in sacrifice probably came from the Black Forest in about 1926, since Heidegger's book, *Sein und Zeit*, first

In the coffee houses they would say it in German—*die Frage*, or *die Seinsfrage*, if they are feeling especially full of themselves.[2] One rule of the coffee house is that one should never say anything in English that could be expressed with greater *gravitas* in a dead language; failing that, use German for the ominous ideas, French for the dismissive ideas, and while Italian is only for the posers too *gauche* to realize that Italian is not *chic*, at least it isn't English.

Returning to "the Question," it is a way of launching a sneak attack on things we already vaguely understand (and presume in our thinking), but which we have failed to make explicit. When we have slunk quietly behind our quarry (the quarry is our own vague awareness), we pop up, say "boo!" and then wait to see what comes running our way. But there are lots of ways to sneak and slink, lots of ways to say "boo!" and still more ways to list and count the things we catch sight of as we flush out the truthy little frightened quails.

In the case of the splendid Dr. Heidegger, he did something he called "fundamental ontology," which outlines the bare essentials one must assume in approaching the Question of Being, oh, wait, I mean *die Seinsfrage*. He transforms that venerable question from "why is there something rather than nothing?" into the slightly less obvious "what sort of being asks such an impossible question?" It turns out, after much hand wringing, that the answer is, "well, the sort of being who asks that question is one that has a *problem* with its own being—and that would be *me*, and maybe also *you*, but definitely me."

But according to Heidegger's zealous and numerous followers, none but the Master himself is deep enough or smart enough to carry out the weighty task of Fundamental Ontology (the capital letters are my own, but I think I can hear them in their tone of voice when I am in the presence of such self-

---

appeared in 1927. The two-part introduction to this work sets out Heidegger's phenomenological method and raises the Question of Being. For a recent translation, see Martin Heidegger, *Being and Time*, trans. Joan Stambaugh (Albany: SUNY Press, 1996), Sections 1–8, 12–36.

[2] Of course, one question leads to another, so if you are very adventurous and would like to investigate the Question surrounding the Question, see Jacques Derrida, *Of Spirit: Heidegger and the Question* (Chicago: University of Chicago Press, 1989).

importance, all of them driving BMW cages in blissful ignorance of the fact that Bayerische Motoren Werke ever even *made* a motorcycle). I am inclined to let the snobs have their Fundamental Ontologies (and if you are one of them, you are not welcome to ride with me, let alone work on my bike) while I go after something more suited to their estimation of *my* depth, or lack thereof (estimation, I mean, not depth).

As William Blake noted, it is a better testament to your character to count some kinds of people among your critics than among your admirers.[3] I think Blake would have fared poorly at a Harley rally, but that doesn't mean he was wrong. His trouble was that he whined about his critics all the time and made enemies needlessly. Perhaps the Blake scholars (and there are many more of these than the world really needs) would be offended, but sometimes I just want to shake some sense into the odd little guy: "Just do the pictures, Bill, write the words. Don't waste your energy on the idiots who don't get it." But no, he couldn't let it go, and so he immortalized his own enemies, none of whose names would even remain to us but for his whining. So I won't bother calling the Heideggerians by name; let history swallow them if it wants to, or me, or both.

Ontological Questions

Ontologies of the sort I want you to consider are motivated by questions. Whenever you find a question that you *know* the answer to, but you don't know *why* you are so sure of yourself, you have the makings of an ontology. But there are so many

---

[3] Blake had lots of ways of saying this, but one of my favorite is: "Thy friendship has oft made my heart to ake: / Do be my Enemy—for Friendship's sake" (*Rosetti MS*, LXXXIV). Another nice one is "To H[ayley]: You think Fuseli is not a Great Painter. I'm Glad./ This is one of the best compliments he ever had." One may find tasty little epigrams like these scattered in Blake's manuscripts that immortalize names such as Flaxman, Cromek, Stothard, Macklin, Boydel, Bowyer, and Hayley that we surely would have lost but for Blake's scribbling complaints. See John Sampson, *The Poetical Works of William Blake* (Williamstown: Corner House, 1978 [1905]), 204–210, 212–16 (*Rosetti MS*, L–LXX, LXXVI–LXXXV). In Blake's defense, he never published these remarks, but he did set them to the page. As for whining, I guess I should go easier on Bill—after all, I was never tried for High Treason. I am confident that it is a drag, and I might whine a little bit myself about that.

questions and so little time. We should choose our questions carefully. I have thought about various possibilities for a guiding question in this chapter. I must have settled on a question or you wouldn't be reading this. I think most people will quickly see that this question has a lot of torque; it is indirect, but it will take us far if we can free ourselves for the trip.

My guiding question is: "Would Bruce Springsteen ride a Honda?"

First off, I don't mean "Has Bruce ever ridden a Honda?" Maybe he has, but ours is not a factual question about Springsteen's biography, it is about two cultural icons, Springsteen and Honda, icons that press upon us an immediate contrast. Our imaginations try to place Bruce on the Honda, and we have a sense of what Walt Disney called the "plausible impossible."[4] We feel we are imagining a fiction when we try to place Bruce on the Honda. We all know Bruce would not "ride a Honda" in the intended iconic sense, even if curiosity or circumstance might have led him actually to try one out at some point. But how do we *know* the answer to this question with such confidence? It seems like a Hog of a question, and everyone knows that taking ownership of a Harley means a commitment to learning how to work on it, but even lesser bikes have maintenance issues. I mean, you don't want to be at the mercy of the guy who owns the repair shop, right? The quality of *his* mercy is pretty strained, nay, it fairly tears a ligament in giving you what you deserve.

In what follows we will first explore this answer to our principal question and collect our insights like needed parts (and I do not mean cheap after-market knock-offs; let the shade-tree mechanics use those—we work only with parts that would make Milwaukee raise a glass—or at least Tokyo), and one by

---

[4] Walt Disney explained the principle of "the plausible impossible" in Episode 55 of *The Wonderful World of Disney*, originally aired on ABC (31st October, 1956)—the series moved to NBC in 1961); it is part two of a trilogy called "The Art of Animation," and is currently available as part of the Walt Disney Treasures DVD set called *Behind the Scenes at the Walt Disney Studios* (dir. A.L. Werker, J. Handley, December 2002), ASIN B00006II6P. For the phenomenological basis of Disney's principle, see Edmund Husserl, *Ideas: General Introduction to Pure Phenomenology* (New York: Humanities Press, 1931), §23, pp. 90–92.

one install them. Eventually we will have a question that purrs, and later we may take it out for a ride, but what more did you really expect? You want the meaning of life? Go see the Dalai Lama.

The Passion of the Boss

Would Bruce ride a Honda? No. But before we can get to the stuff that is so boss about the answer, we need to spend some time tinkering with the question while we're still in the onto-logical living room (yes, we work on this bike in the living room, not in the garage; if you are worried about the mess, go read a different chapter). Put on some old clothes in case you get substances on yourself.

We learn much about the value of the question when we imagine variations. Ontologists always imagine variations.[5] I think the question needs to be formulated just as it is, and not, for example, "would Bruce ride a Harley?" to which the answer is "duh." That question leads us nowhere we have not already been, many times, although maybe we could have an interest-ing chat about what model Harley Bruce *should* ride, if you only knew more about it. The question also cannot be "would Woody Guthrie ride a Honda?" which is a jarring enough ques-tion, but I fear it is too great a project for any but Heidegger and his most profound followers. Indeed, that Woody Guthrie ques-tion is just one short step away from the *Seinsfrage*.

A much more predictable conversation could be had if we asked "would Jesus ride a Honda or a Harley?" To this one, we can all agree he wouldn't ride a Honda (see below), but I fear we would be split over the Harley question, with a small minor-ity insisting not only that Jesus *would* ride a Harley, but that he actually *did* enter Jerusalem on a Hog (which may explain why things soon started looking like Glen Hanson's demise in *Easy Rider*—am I the only one who has noticed the similarity between that scene and Mel Gibson's *Passion of the Christ*?).

---

[5] For an explanation of the method of imaginative variation, see Husserl, *ibid.*, §§68–70, pp. 195–201. For an explanation of the explanation (trust me, you'll need it), see Erazim Kohák, *Idea and Experience: Edmund Husserl's Project of Phenomenology in* Ideas I (Chicago: University of Chicago Press, 1978), pp. 143–47.

This is my own view, in fact; not that Jesus *would* ride a Harley, but that he actually *did*. But let's keep it light. I think we can easily agree on the Bruce part of the question. Maybe Jesus on a Harley, definitely Bruce, no Honda for either one.

The "Honda" part of the question is equally crucial. It's an uncomfortable truth that there are two manufacturers of real motorcycles in the world today. One is Harley-Davidson, the other is Honda. The rest are wanna-be's. I am not saying Suzuki and Yamaha have made no real bikes. They made and make inferior Hondas.[6] I am not saying BSA, Triumph, Norton, and Indian never made real bikes. They made and make inferior Harleys.[7] Here is another uncomfortable truth: Honda knows how to make a motorcycle.[8] Hondas are fast, they are efficient, they last forever, they require very little maintenance, and yes, they even look good (to the middle-class, suburban eye). After

---

[6] I use the word "inferior" advisedly, being well aware of the excellence of some other bikes, especially Yamahas. Honda and Yamaha fought it out for world pre-eminence among the Japanese manufacturers in a war that nearly buried Harley-Davidson in the early 1980s, but I speak here not of the specific history but of the battle for supremacy in the public mind, for the status of "cultural icon." If this were a matter of history rather than philosophy we might pursue these issues, but my claim has to do with things everyone knows, which is that history has proclaimed Honda the victor, regardless of whether there may be some Yamahas that were in some sense superior. That's why "Yamaha" is a friggin' piano in the mind of John Q. Much has been written on this historic battle between Honda and Yamaha, but for something suitably compact, see Greg Field's short essay "H-D vs. Japan," in *The Harley-Davidson Century*, edited by Darwin Holstrom (St. Paul: MBI, 2004), pp. 206–07. I certainly confess that Suzuki, Kawasaki, and Yamaha have made some impressive crotch-rockets, but the later agreements with Erik Buell have lifted Harley into a position of great respect even among the sport-bike enthusiasts. Buell and Harley certainly are of a feather, even if H-D was slower to recognize Buell's genius as an engineer than they should have been.

[7] As above, this is a matter of the historical outcome in the battle for cultural supremacy, not a judgment about technical achievement or actual history, regarding which more subtlety of argument is needed.

[8] I do not deny that a wealth of literature and judgment exists from Harley partisans that trashes the quality of Hondas, but there is a more balanced and sober literature that recognizes in the words of Greg Field, "Soichiro Honda's genius," and while Field specifically had in mind the electric starter in saying this, he adds that Honda knew "motorcycles would never appeal to the masses until they were just . . . as reliable as a car" (*The Harley-Davidson Century*, p. 127).

some initial experiments, Harley-Davidson made the decision soon after Hondas appeared in the U.S. market not even to compete, and Honda reciprocated (initially at least).[9] It was a sign of mutual respect, and while Harley-Davidson learned some lessons from Japan, and taught Japan as many, H-D also showed a great awareness of what makes a Harley a Harley, that ineffable something (that *je ne sais quoi*, if you need a phrase to go with your cappuccino) that would be lost if certain paths were followed. Harley-Davidson was unwilling to make McMotorcycles. It is worth noting that Honda also makes the best cages in the world. Harley-Davidson will not be trying to compete there either. Our first needed parts in this rebuild project: most battles are won or lost in the choosing, and there is no dishonor in letting someone else make a buck you never needed anyway. How different corporate America would be if it grasped this lesson!

Thus, I claim, we ask "would Springsteen ride a *Honda?*" precisely because it's the most informative contrast available to us. Honda makes an outstanding bike and they always did. The question is about a profound relation between, on the one side, very defensible, conservative, thrifty middle-class values and on the other side, well, a somewhat impractical craving for freedom from those same values (not to reject them wholesale, but to take or leave them, as conscience and the sense of self may demand).

So what does Honda mean? Again, we seek contrast. By way of illustration, for instance, we intuitively recognize the ridiculousness of a Honda with extended forks. There are some things that just ought not be tricked out, like June Cleaver in a thong and pasties or a Honda 750 with extended forks (the 750 is still the "manliest" bike Honda ever made, but even *it* is something that could be respectably featured in an article for *Redbook*). The Honda as an icon helps us understand that this is a contrast not just of values, but of fundamental—even existential—relations. The truth is that Bruce could never *love* a Honda with all the madness in his soul, and the reason can be summed up in this phrase: Honda cannot make a suicide machine.

---

[9] The history is complicated, but again, please refer to Greg Field, "H-D vs. Japan" in *The Harley-Davidson Century*, pp. 206–07.

Honda cannot make a suicide machine because that would contradict every value they have poured into their bikes from the first. In fact, this is part of the reason we all know Jesus wouldn't have ridden a Honda. He had no use for middle-class values of this sort. What we may disagree on is whether he went into Jerusalem in a final act of defiance and there committed suicide willingly by the hands of others. But *if* he did that, he did it on a Harley, because a Harley is not first and foremost a bike or even a machine. A Harley is a *decision* about life and what makes it valuable, and how it needs to be lived. When that decision comes to be embodied and epitomized in a machine, we *call* it a Harley. Here we have another needful part: Harley-Davidson, as cultural icon, represents not a machine first or foremost, but an existential decision and the life that follows upon it. We will seek to understand that decision and the philosophies that accompany it in the next chapter, when we hit the road, but we are not quite finished tinkering with this question. We have seen "it's not just a bike, it's a choice," but have we understood it?

The Moment of Truth (or Falsehood)

A narrative may help to bring this point into greater relief. With your indulgence, I want to rehearse a scene from my own youth that has been replayed tens of millions of times in other lives in the last forty years, with incidental variations. Many of you will recognize the story. My father, like so many men of his generation, rose to become a successful professional from a humble background. He capitulated in 1975 (after much cajoling, maybe even a little whining) to my adolescent pleas for a motorcycle. Like any father of that day and age, he would "make this a learning process" for me. I would learn about all the different motorcycles available, within a determined price and power range, and then we would make an informed purchase. After reading the available materials, a Wednesday was designated during which we would visit each dealership, but we would not be buying a motorcycle *that* day—this was made perfectly clear. We would narrow our choices and return to the dealers whose offerings impressed us, and we would pay a fair price, and we would *know* what a fair price was. Such were the preordained values. And while the best trade plans of micely men can sometimes turn askew, sometimes they don't.

Now, there are two types of fathers in such situations: there are those who *take* their sons to the Harley-Davidson dealership, and then there are fathers who are willing to be *taken* there. No father who consents to having an adolescent son of his on a bike at all is likely to *rule out* the Harley in advance. Those Harley-less fathers and the ones who simply say "no" to their sons' pleas for a bike are the same class of fathers. *Their* sons, on account of the fathers' restrictions, will eventually learn on their own (or spend the rest of life wishing they had), that it takes a minimum of two men to bring a boy to manhood, and that the *boy* chooses the second man, not the father. Saying "no" to a son who is serious about his request for a bike is a fast way to insure that the boy will choose a mentor whose values are quite unlike his father's; he will certainly choose a mentor whom his father would reject, perhaps for the very reason that his father *would* reject such a spirit guide. Fathers reading this, be advised: If the boy wants a bike, you will do well to make that possible for him. If your girl wants a bike, best of luck. I have no advice for you. Girls on bikes and girls on horses are all quite appealing—even unappealing women become strangely intriguing astride a great beast or a great machine, for reasons I would do better not to investigate too closely, but I have the sense that it is for the girl and her mother to work out the wherefores.

My own father was willing to be *taken* to the Harley dealership. The one quirk in my personal narrative is that the episode occurred during the one year that H-D offered a 90cc bike.[10] In some ways, 1975 was the pivotal year not only for me, but for Harley-Davidson and Honda, because the territory of the imaginations of American mass culture was being divvied up at just that moment, and my own decision about a bike illustrated the moment pretty nicely. A few years before, Honda had introduced its SL 70cc enduro bike (street legal, but suitable for trail

---

[10] This bike, the Z90, was actually made by Aermacchi, an Italian manufacturer with which H-D collaborated for a number of years after 1960. It was quickly apparent that competing with the Japanese on smaller models was a losing proposition in many senses for H-D, and the 90cc bike was never offered again, nor was there anything else smaller than 54ci until after 1995. See *The Encyclopedia of the Harley-Davidson* by Peter Henshaw and Ian Kerr (Edison: Chartwell Books, 2004), p. 172.

riding, which was then a growing craze), and Harley had entered the fray with the 90cc enduro bike made by Aermacchi. The latter bore the Harley name, however, and the name already meant what it still means today.

But I Digress

I will return to my narrative in a moment, but we have a bolt stuck here and we need an impact wrench. Peter Fonda's "Captain America" seems to have clinched the iconic standing of the Harley, which had long been associated with a certain conception of freedom and individualism, but in the wake of *Easy Rider*, the popular imagination had crystallized around this idea. Part of the genius of Captain America was its symbolic insistence upon the association of patriotism with this very notion of freedom and individualism—this bike gave us permission to think for ourselves about *what* devotion and loyalty to the ideals of America really means, and the irony that this bike conveyed its rider towards making a drug deal (outside of the current laws) is also a source of creative tension. Brilliant. It's worth pausing to consider how Dennis Hopper's film and its impact would have been different if Fonda had ridden *any* other bike (not just a non-Harley, but even any Harley other than Captain America). It is dangerous to make assertions about "might-have-beens," or what analytic philosophers like to call "counterfactuals," because no evidence can exist that fully demonstrates the falseness of such assertions. But with that disclaimer noted, I want to suggest that the film becomes close to meaningless without the rolling American flag. That bike is the iconic key to the kingdom, not only of that one film, but to the kingdom of America the Paradoxical. It is not an accident that our celluloid sacrificial lamb, Glen Hanson, is a rogue lawyer incognito, and that, symbolically, it is precisely the *law* that suffers a brutal death at the hands of those who believe themselves to be defending it and its ideals, because, after all, the letter kills the spirit, according to Jesus, just as surely as the rednecks kill Glen Hanson.

The Story of the Moral

Predictably, the Honda and the Harley were the finalists in my father's version of bowling-for-buddy-pegs. The Wednesday for purchasing arrived, about as slowly as Christmas (another notion we wouldn't have without Jesus, not so much Christmas, but the idea that it is slow—he sure took his sweet time showing up, what with Babylonians and Assyrians running amuck, and all those depressing lamentations, I mean, incarnate already, would ya? Christ in a sidecar!).

We went to the Honda dealership first. Immediately the salesman (wrongly) guessed that the decision would actually rest with my father. He proceeded to explain the practicality of the (new) XL 70, its four-stroke engine, its low maintenance requirements, its reliability, its lower price, its superior resale value, its safety features (he even dared to offer my father the optional governor for the carburetor that would keep me below 35 mph). Upon learning that the Harley was his competitor in our case, he freely trashed it. "That Dago junker? . . ." he said, after checking my dad's card to make sure our name wasn't Delvecchio or Altabello. The Honda dealer had an impressive command of the factors bearing upon WASPish middle-class values, and an equally impressive set of prejudices to back them up. But he also had a pretty good little bike.

At the Harley dealership, the salesman was a biker. He correctly surmised within two or three minutes of observing me and my father that the decision was actually *mine* to make, although my father had never said as much to me—I guess dad was watching to see what I would do, and the biker recognized it. My Harley salesman was therefore speaking to a fourteen-year-old kid. He never had a bad word to say about the Honda XL 70. He was asking me what I *wanted* without making comparisons. I learned that the Harley was quite powerful, had a much higher top-end speed, and I already knew it was cooler by far. Without saying so, the Harley salesman helped me understand that this decision was about who I was and wanted to be. The Harley had a two-stroke engine, requiring me to mix the oil and gas. It sat higher off the ground. It was very cool. I still want a Z90.

I chose the Honda (without the governor, thank you very much, top speed of 50 m.p.h.). I apologize to the readers who would have wished for the opposite choice. If I had chosen the Harley, someone else would be writing this chapter, or maybe no one would write it. I would be doing something else, or be dead. To make matters worse, I subsequently chose five or six more Hondas over the next thirty years (more about that in the next chapter). My father would have allowed the Harley choice and supported it, but his personal values had been imparted to me without being forced on me, and he was pleased with my choice. I could tell.

And I was actually honest with myself—in the sense that I realized I could not self-honestly ride a Harley. I already liked Peter, Paul and Mary and Don McLean better than Led Zeppelin and the Stones, and I secretly thought Steppenwolf was very noisy. Would I compensate for my own sentimentality with a big bike, or just confess it? I belong on a Honda. I am pleased that I look just as comfortable on a ratty Honda as on a sleek new one, but a Honda it must be. I always admired the guys who *belonged* on the Harleys and I wanted their friendship. And I detested the guys who chose Harleys and did not deserve to ride them.[11] It quickly became evident to me that there is room in the world of loyal bikers for a guy who belongs on a Honda, so long as he knows who he is and does not pose or make a fool of himself by lying to others or to himself about it. This is the part we need to get our bike running, that and our metric ontological tools, for, as you can see, we've been working on a Honda. I just put it in the living room to scare you.

But that Harley dealer could see that I did not care how the motorcycle really worked, I just wanted the ride. He did not say "buy the Honda," but he knew I would. I was headed for the coffee house already. I can easily recall that the reason I gave myself at the time was that the Harley sat a little too high off the ground (in retrospect, the symbolism of that seems right), and that the two-stroke engine would be a hassle. What kind of kid is deterred from buying his first Harley by a two-

---

[11] So I wrote this essay mainly while camping at the Kerrville Folk Festival in May and June of 2005 (which should be pretty telling, I mean, it's not exactly Daytona), and parked down in the recently added RV lots is this guy with the biggest RV I have ever seen, and I walk by one day and he's got this tricked out purple Harley parked by his home-away-from-home (I am well aware of this practice at the actual rallies, but hear me out). So I pause as he is loung-ing by his rolling Biltmore, drinking a pretty pricey pinot noir: "Nice RV," I say, with ascending intonation. A pause. "Thanks," said he. Another pause. "Nice Harley," descending intonation, just a hint of a sigh. I walk on. I'm thinking, "I wonder how he pulls that RV with 54ci. . . ." Enough said.

stroke engine? The sort of kid who needs to be riding a Honda and buying Don McLean records. This is not merely about convenience or predilection, it is about identity, sense of self, core values.

It's true that some choose to serve appearances in making such decisions, some chasing after what they believe *others* will see as "cool," others attempting to please the expectations of a parent. Such persons will have more complicated journeys to self-understanding than those who confront the decision for what it truly is. The ones who choose their rides based on appearances have been consumed in what Heidegger calls the "they self," or in German (since this is a very ominous idea) *das Man*, which is the self that conceals its own fundamental modes of existing in order to live inauthentically, caught up in the world of images and slogans and RVs. Bikers have more straightforward terms for such people, such as "assholes," but the nomenclature isn't crucial here. We will leave such persons to the things they believe are important. But in the domain of those who confront existential issues more directly, Robert Frost would have appreciated the depth of the choice between a Harley and a Honda and would have been able to summarize it better. For me, the road *more* traveled was the right call, but it still leaves one many delightful miles to go before one sleeps.

Yes, this seems to be the spare part we needed to get our question running. I might be too lazy to mix gas and oil, but there is more than one kind of laziness. We haven't been lazy about our question. Let's check it over, see if this beast will start before we take it on the open road. We asked: would Bruce ride a Honda? We knew he would not. We considered variations on the question. We discovered that Bruce and Jesus have something in common, which can be summarized as: "live free or die," as they say in New Hampshire. Both Jesus and Bruce have a *passion*, meaning they are open to the world, a certain intense ontological longing, they "want to know love is wild" and "want to know if love is real." That mode of existing, the "passion of the Boss," is compatible with mounting a suicide machine, whether it takes one to the "mansions of glory," or Highway 9, or Sturgis, or Golgotha. The cultural ontology of the suicide machine shows us some-

3

The Biker Bar and the Coffee House: A Paean to the Postmodern Pagans

RANDALL E. AUXIER

Getting It Started

We settled in the last chapter that *you* probably belong in a coffee house, but you've got a wild hair, so you're living dangerously, willing to slum it for a chapter or two. So be it. I'll put up with you for a few more pages if you ask nicely.

It would be so easy to say, "the hedonists inhabit the biker bars and the idealists are in the coffee houses," and this is not entirely wrong; it conveys the kind of truth that other sorts of hackneyed generalizations have—they became hackneyed for a reason. In this case, it is sort of like saying "there are animals in the zoo and fish at the aquarium." Generally speaking, yes. It's not very informative, and indeed, it's far more fun to *go* to the zoo and the aquarium than to give a taxonomy from a distance of their likely contents, especially at the abstract level of sub-kingdom. In philosophy, hedonists and idealists are like sub-kingdoms (about equally plentiful, but with little intersection of habitat). *Of course* there are idealists in coffee houses and hedonists in biker bars, but why? What kinds? Why can I become a coffee house hero with my Marxist invective when the same speech will only get my ass kicked in a biker bar?

Let's begin by noting: no Marxist would be unwelcome in a biker bar *just* for being a Marxist; there are some socialists and even a few Marxists to be found in biker bars. Che Guevara rode a bike. But biker revolutionaries know to keep that sort of thing to themselves, as does most everyone else in the biker bar. The trouble with your coffee-house revolutionary is that he is usually a dweeb without common sense enough to realize that a part of "live and let live" is "think and let think," which means don't shoot off your mouth unless you intend to do something about it, you pencil-neck. . . . Sorry. I am way ahead of myself.

What follows is mainly for the coffee house dweller who has always wanted to grasp something about bikers and the bikes they ride, but who has been too far on the outside of that culture to learn much about it. You can't actually get this down without experiencing it all first-hand, but assuming it is not practical for you to hop a Harley and ride as a way of life, perhaps the figurative ride we take in this chapter will serve as a substitute, albeit a pale and wordy one. Those who already know the culture of bikes and bikers may not learn as much from what I have to say, but I suspect there are some things written here that they may have understood vaguely for many years without ever bringing them into expressed form. If there is value in this chapter for bikers themselves, it will be in the pleasure of recognition, or perhaps in the pleasure of disagreement with my generalizations and conclusions. I hope none of you will be disappointed, but in any case strap your hands across my engines while we get out of town (with or without the bones from our backs).

Half the Journey

This beast starts. Some will ask "where are we going?" Those inquirers need to stay at home. It would be ridiculous to suppose we *need* a destination before we hit the road. There are no Aristotelians in the biker bars and precious few in coffee houses (where they are disliked, but they do order the more expensive concoctions, the double full nelson *latte* mocha with sprinkles and whipped cream—keeps the place in business, you know). Aristotelians believe the journey does not *mean* anything unless the purpose and end is already present in the beginning. Those sorts of people need to serve their bureaucracies and then die their meaningless deaths. They never want to admit that the one universal end and destination for all life is death. I would rather "do lunch" with a BMW-driving Heideggerian. These Aristotelians who fill our cities find death uncomfortable, and instead say that things like flourishing and health and happiness are the prescribed ends of human life. They conveniently explain away the observation that flourishing and happiness are at best transient conditions of a process that marches inexorably towards the grave, and they vote for Republicans and Democrats, convincing themselves there is some sort of difference between the two. Those who will take this ride with us are untroubled about the *fact* of dying and do not expect happiness or flourishing. For us the question is how well shall we live and how well shall we die. When this question is understood deeply, we stop competing with the Joneses and find our churches beyond the walls of Aristotelian acceptability. Heaven becomes for us not a destination but a relation between what is, what has been, and what will be. The Kingdom of Heaven is within, I think Springsteen once said. Or was it Kerouac? Anyway, it was right.

I know a place called the Iron Post just a few hours away from town where we can stop. We can worry about the rest later, or maybe not.

It's Okay, I'm with the Band

In many hours spent in conversation with bikers, I have come to think that their genuine variety is often underestimated by the conservative middle class. I am not interested in trying to rid the suburbanites of their ignorance or in reorganizing their prejudices. But I do think that one thing I've never seen attempted is a sketch of the philosophical schools into which bikers most often fall. In spite of my own preference for Hondas, I spent a lot of time in biker bars as a musician—bikers love music, all kinds—and I was privileged to befriend many fine philosophers there who would not have darkened the door of a college. The band gets a privileged look inside the world of biker culture, basically because of that soft spot for music. No matter how geeky you may be, if you can wail on a Strat or thump a bass or pound those skins, you are welcome at the biker bar. Indeed, unlike other folks, musicians actually get the benefit of the doubt and not only are well-treated, but protected from the usual rough and tumble. It is part of a complicated unspoken web of *mores*, or social rules, that I can more easily illustrate than explain. The illustration comes later in this trip. But suffice to say, like many other musicians, I learned what I learned about bikers from the vantage of the bandstand; recall that the band is the first to arrive and the last to leave.

And Try Not to Embarrass Yourself

Before we get to the Iron Post, there are a few basics we need to be clear about so that we don't cause any trouble. Our steed is up and running but remember, it may be a Harley-*sized* question we asked in the last chapter, but it's really a big Gold Wing touring bike. The fellows who ride the Harleys don't put much stock in such questions. So we are riding a Honda over to the other side. We don't actually fit in very well at the bar, but we will be welcome enough as long as we don't behave like the coffee-house jerks we actually are.

Rule number one is reserve your judgment about the choices and lifestyles of others until you have walked a mile in their shoes, no, ten miles, or better yet, just reserve your judgment indefinitely. You will never fully understand why they are the way they are, even after spending years getting to know them, so save your high-handed judgments for another time and place, or if you want to get yourself on the path to true wisdom, let this experience be the beginning of a therapy that will enable you to let all that judgment leave your troubled mind for keeps. There is enough to worry about in this world without adding your uninformed opinions about how other people live to that pile.

Second, I especially need you to bite your tongue regarding what you will see as the misogyny of this lifestyle. That issue is very complicated. Our opinions will not change the facts and our judgments will not affect the practices. Is this a patriarchal subculture built upon the logic of domination and the objectification of women, consumed with self-absorbed machismo? Perhaps. Get used to it. No one forces anyone into this kind of life. Spare us your crypto-paternalism regarding how some young girls might be seduced by false promises. If you start talking this way when we are at the Iron Post, I may just leave you there.

A third thing to grasp is that philosophy is more enacted than propounded in the biker bar. In the coffee house, it is the reverse, of course. Plenty of the good folks we find at the Iron Post could talk a coffee-house dweeb in circles, if they wanted to, but they don't. The best course of action is to buy a beer, sit back, observe without obtruding, and talk to whomever decides to talk to us. If we sit with an obvious open spot at the table and comfortable, nonjudgmental countenances, plenty of interesting people might talk to us. Bikers are generally both gregarious and curious, close observers and generous spirits.

Finally, you must understand that you *will* accept whatever hospitality is offered, no matter how peculiar the offer may be. It is not uncommon for the first approach to our sort (and they will know what sort we are) to be calculated to determine whether we are . . . well, I'll use Heidegger's terms . . . persons given over to the shallow and inauthentic form of self-experience. If you are offered something to drink, drink it. If you are offered something to smoke, smoke it. It can get stranger than that, but you get the idea. Our future friends will ask for an expression of both trust and openness before any exchange will occur. You will not be harmed simply for being uncool and ill at ease, and if you want to be trusted, you have to trust. Alright, here we are, at the Iron Post. Let us go inside and order something to drink.

Philosophy at the Biker Bar

It occurred to me, years after I traded in my electric bass for an acoustic guitar, that there really is something in the history of philosophy that would serve as a fair scheme of classifying the philosophers I have known who ride Harleys (and belong on them). The scheme follows almost precisely the standard schools of Hellenistic Platonism. Don't ask me why. I think there is probably a real connection between bikers and pagans, but whether I could actually trace the genealogy that way I don't know. Let the analogy suffice for now and you can get historical if you need to on your own time. Here, roughly, then, are the four philosophies I have seen developed and expounded over beers.

Epicureanism, or the Dancing Biker

If you're comfortable enough, leave a space there at the end of our table nearest to the bar, and turn the chair part-way out. The fellow who owns this place goes by the name of Cowboy. He

picked that name up in Nam, where he was a chopper pilot,
U.S. Army Cavalry. He has a master's degree in mechanical engineering. Some bikers have fancy educations, some do not, but
none regards the degree as designating anything of great importance. That's just a piece of paper. What it means in concrete
terms, if it means anything at all, is that not only can Cowboy
fix just about anything, he can create all sorts of contraptions to
do just about anything he wants done. He opened this place
about twenty years ago with his old lady Rose (they have been
together since before the war). They have a good business sense
and know how to keep things light. Cowboy is an Epicurean,
which is just about my favorite sort of biker.

Epicurus[1] lived from 341 to 270 B.C.E. and came from a beautiful island called Samos (more bicycles than bikes there). In
about 307 he established a little community called The Garden.
It was a place where his friends could gather, enjoy wine,
cheese, conversation, and music. He believed that the best way
to live was to pursue the kinds of worldly pleasures that are
most sustainable and that lead to the least trouble and pain.
Moderation is not an absolute requirement, but it is wise advice.
Epicurus did not think the gods were sufficiently interested in
human affairs to bother to intervene or even take note of our
distress or joy. It is up to us to make for ourselves the best of
our human lot. Chance is something very real in the universe,
but we can minimize its negative impact on us by shielding ourselves from the aspects of life in which chance runs roughshod
over people's aspirations to happiness, such as politics, business
deals, and deep involvement in the outcome of struggles for
power. A certain willingness to withdraw from that sort of stuff
will give a person the best possible shot at a good life.

For Cowboy and Rose, the Iron Post is not a money-making
establishment, it is not an investment; it is a space where life can
happen. Striving to keep it open and hospitable, protected from
overzealous law enforcement or the world of jerks, is what
Cowboy and Rose want. They create an atmosphere in which
people look out for each other, in which friends will prevent
friends from saying words that damage the honor and dignity of

---

[1] Pronounce the first part like "hepatitis" and the second part like what we
want the doctor to do to everyone who has it.

others such that only violence can restore the balance. By years of selfless service to this community they nurture, Cowboy and Rose have cultivated a deep, deep loyalty among both the regulars and the infrequent visitors to their place. They used to stay out back in a very livable trailer, but now they have a little land just down the valley from here.

I wish I could make this less cryptic for you, but the only way to understand why Cowboy is an Epicurean is to tell you what decisions he has made in his life, and the most significant decisions are really summed up in, well, his bikes. Cowboy has two bikes. He has a vintage 49E Hydra-Glide, 61ci, V-twin, medium compression, four-speed, restored to the original peacock blue. His father bought it new in '49. His workhorse is a 73FX Super Glide, 74ci, V-twin four-speed. He has rebuilt that bike so many times we all lost count. For a while it seemed like he was rebuilding it every winter, but I think it finally hit the perfect balance about 1990. Cowboy bought that bike when he was discharged from the service in '73, made the down payment with his last paycheck from Uncle Sam. Cowboy usually takes the '49 to Sturgis, and not in an RV and not on a trailer, if you get my drift. I hear he blesses the four directions with tobacco and says some words for his old man the day he arrives. In earlier years Cowboy would always go on a bender the first night in Sturgis, and that is the only time you could get him to talk about Nam, but not so much any more. He has owned a few other bikes as projects over the years, but he never had any serious intention of keeping them. He sent them to good homes with guys he liked, probably at a loss, but he hadn't bothered to keep track of the time or money he had into them. One bike that Cowboy rebuilt was an especially sweet Shovelhead, about a 1980 I think (anyway, it was one of the last Big Twins), that he gave to Gary, who still bounces for him at the Iron Post. I will tell you about Gary later, but they knew each other in the Army. Gary and Cowboy rebuilt that bike together and Gary had no idea Cowboy was going to give it to him. It was a surprise on Gary's anniversary of ten years sober.

I hope I don't have to paint a picture for you. If you cannot see from what I have said that Cowboy is an Epicurean, you need to just stop here and ask yourself what sort of man makes the decisions Cowboy has made and why. He isn't going to spell it out for you and neither am I. What I will say is that I have known a fair number of bikers like Cowboy, and the world isn't big enough to contain my respect for them. You will see that everyone else around here feels the same way. If a disrespectful word about Cowboy ever leaves your lips, there will be a long line of people waiting to kick your ass, but the irony is, Cowboy wouldn't let us. He would remind us after you leave that you were hardly worth the effort, even if it would have been fun. Then we'll party.

Skepticism (Pyrrhonian), or the Quiet Biker

The big fellow over there at the bar is called Bear. I think his real name is Charles but no one calls him that, and I don't advise you to call him either Bear or Charles unless someone he knows introduces you. He won't be joining us at our table. Cowboy almost certainly will, if he comes in, and so will Gary, but not Bear. Don't worry, he neither likes you nor dislikes you; in fact he doesn't give a tinker's damn about you one way or the other. He has no reason to, does he? The teat that provides the milk of human kindness dried up some time in the Sixties as far as he is concerned, so you are on your own, and so is everybody else. Don't expect any help from Bear; he certainly won't be asking for your help. Bear has a whole lifetime of lessons learned from first-hand experience that he won't be sharing with you or anyone else. Whatever path you think you might want to try, he probably already tried it and knows just where it leads. One thing he has learned is that nearly all people *think* they know more than they do. Bear is a skeptic.

Skepticism is a Hellenistic school of thought that came to be divided into two main kinds, the Academic Skeptics, sometimes called "Carneadean" after their most influential spokesman, Carneades (around 213–128 B.C.E.),[2] and the followers of Sextus Empiricus (approximately 275–350 C.E., I mean, these are skeptics, so who knows?).[3] Sextus claimed to be following Pyrrho of Elis (around 360–270 B.C.E.),[4] and so he and his gang were called "Pyrrhonian Skeptics."

---

[2] Pronounced like some sort of gum disease endured by the transient workers at the local Midway, "carni-a-deez."

[3] A forerunner of Professor Alfred C. Kinsey.

[4] Pronunciation hint: imagine a trip to the famous Pier 39 in San Francisco,

The difference is important. I do not believe there are any followers of Carneades in the biker bar, and I don't think there are any followers of Pyrrho in the coffee houses. Similarly, no Pyrrhonian would ride a Honda, and if a Carneadean rides a Harley, he does so as a fool (probably hauls it in an RV). What, then, is this crucial difference? I don't want to oversimplify it, but I also don't want to belabor it, so I will make a sweeping generalization that captures the essence of the difference: Carneadeans do not doubt the *value* of knowledge, only the possibility of obtaining it; while Pyrrhonians do not focus on the possibility of knowledge so much as whether the human possession of knowledge, even if it were possible, would make us any better off. If we ask a Pyrrhonian "can humans possess true knowledge?" the answer would be "probably not, but what makes you assume it would even be a *good* thing to have?" On balance, what we humans have been wont to call "knowledge" does at least as much harm as good, and it never has lived up to its billing as the key to virtue, according to the Pyrrhonians.

The coffee house Carneadean likes to bait the lovers of knowledge into endless controversy about how they *know* what they claim to know and is able to do so because everyone in the coffee house *wants* knowledge and freely assumes everyone is better off with knowledge than without it. The Pyrrhonians have thought further than this, recognizing that if all claims to know are shipwrecked on the jagged rocks off the coast of Being, then maybe the best life for mortals is *not* a life that requires "knowledge." Perhaps the lesson is that we mortals should cultivate a suspension of judgment or *epoche* (but don't use that word here, save it for the coffee house), by which we can stifle our own pointless curiosity. How much does a person need to know to live well? Not much, if history is any teacher, but the principal item of knowledge that does seem relevant to happiness is the mindfulness of limitations on judgments of both what is known and what is good.

Bear is not going to argue with you about whether you know what you are talking about. It isn't worth his time. That doesn't mean he has no opinion. It means he is generally content to let you crash your own bike. He does not celebrate when you do,

---

hang a right at the sea lions and walk past 38 more. The next pier on the left, if there were any, would be your skeptical guy.

but he doesn't feel sorry for you either. The one subject he *will* become verbal about is the discussion of various bikes. Bear has ridden a lot of different bikes over the years and he complains about every one of them. He has never had a bike that suited him. He can tell you in detail the about design flaws in every Harley model since about 1970, and he has a special, almost transcendent contempt for the twin cam engine.

In about '98 he showed up at the Iron Post on a BSA. I don't even know what model it is, but he still rides it when it is running. That bike gives him more trouble than any Hog he ever had, but he makes a point of praising its design when he has had a few beers. I suspect it is pure contrariness on his part, but I'm certainly not going to argue with him. What do I care? It's not like he is impressed by *my* bike, and he won't exactly welcome a lifelong Honda devotee's opinion of the Harleys he is so fond of criticizing. Bear has been through nearly as many women as bikes, and he can tell you all of their design flaws too. He swore off women about the same time he bought that BSA, but he was a little late, since, from what I have heard, women had sworn him off a few months earlier. Bear is not happy, but at least he doesn't expect to be. Stay clear of him when he starts drinking Jack straight. He is a very mean drunk, but fortunately it doesn't happen all that often. Bear is a great companion for a long ride, especially if you aren't looking for conversation. He doesn't know much, but neither do you, frankly.

Bear is untroubled by convention and lives just a little bit beyond good and evil, having a tendency to shift his standards as needed to fit the situation. He is not actually self-centered or stubborn but he sometimes seems like it. You should give him wide berth. Even his peers have gotten to know him only over many years, and they will be the first to say they don't really know what makes him tick. You will never get to know him or understand what makes him tick. Stop trying to figure it out. He isn't dangerous unless you do something stupid. He thinks Dylan should have died in that crash since he hasn't given the world anything worth having since about '66, and he isn't too sure about before that either. Bear doesn't want to live long enough to become his own biographer like Dylan did.

Cynicism (includes Hedonism), Like a True Nature's Child

I want to tell you about my friend Happy Jack, well, he really isn't my friend except when he wants something, but anyway, he is a cynic—I don't see him here at the Iron Post right now, but he may turn up later—my point is that before I tell you about Jack, I have to explain something. Let me approach this indirectly: One of my favorite lines from the days of true Rock and Roll (the vicinity of 1968) was in the chorus of "Born to Be Wild":

Like a true nature's child, we were born, born to be wild

In the coffee house the first thing likely to be noticed is that there seems to be a grammatical issue with pronoun number, but that shows how little they know in the coffee house. John Kay (née Joachim Krauledat, a weird name even in German), who wrote that song, *may* have been reading his Heidegger and Jung—but he was certainly reading his Hermann Hesse, and if you do not know why I say so, perhaps you should look him up before you start correcting his grammar. If there is one thing that bugs me about coffee house philosophers it is their habit of thinking they understand something before they really do, always rushing to *appear* knowledgeable to others and prizing not quite highly enough the difficult process by which genuine knowledge is obtained, a process called *empiria* in one dead language they revere more than study. The nature's child is an imaginative universal, an archetype, and our participation in it is collective. The grammar is exact. Not only is the nature's child the most pervasive embodied philosophy in the biker bar, it is the most easily misunderstood. If images of sprites and druids and wood nymphs are leaping to your mind when you hear the phrase "nature's child," that is understandable but somewhat jarring when considering the population of the Iron Post. Not one wood nymph here to be seen. But there is more than one way to understand "nature's child," and the applicable path in this case is by way of Cynicism.

There are all kinds of cynics in the biker bar, as many shades and degrees as there are breeds of dogs. The word "cynic" even comes from the Greek word for dog, *kuon*, and it was the nickname given to one Diogenes of Sinope (fourth century B.C.E.), who not only questioned the conventional values of the Hellenistic world but also lived in public defiance of those values. Our actual information about him is very sketchy, anecdotal, shrouded in the mists of legend, but somehow that seems quite right.

Diogenes pronounced himself a "citizen of the universe," which was easier than pronouncing his name, professing loyalty to no state (it is not surprising perhaps that he was exiled from his native Sinope, and constantly in trouble in Athens and Corinth). Diogenes was said to carry around a lantern even during the day. When asked why, he replied he was looking for an honest man amid the depraved cities. It is said that when Alexander the Great sought out Diogenes, having heard of his wisdom, Diogenes asked Alexander to get out of his lantern light, with the evident implication that Alexander was certainly not the honest man Diogenes sought. Diogenes lived to tell the tale, and apparently Alexander left at least one world unconquered, viz., the inner world (he might still have wept at the prospect, since the territory is so vast). Other anecdotes about Diogenes defecating publicly in the marketplace, or pleasuring himself whenever and wherever the urge struck, or wearing a barrel because he rejected the conventions associated with clothing, and the like, may or may not be factual. What is important is that convention had no hold over Diogenes and he believed that human beings were essentially animals whose happiness lay in learning how to live self-sufficiently *as* animals. Conventions and "high culture" simply filled the human head with nothing but lies and trash of a sort that leads an animal to grief, or to take pleasure in depravities, or to desire power and wealth with which to control others.

This is where we must proceed carefully. There is a certain sense in which cynics seem hedonistic—by conventional standards, that is—and a different sense in which they seem ascetic. For example, cynics are likely to eschew luxuries, delicacies, and debaucheries that emerge from human power games, from the moneychase that *is* corporate capitalism, and the like. But these voluntary deprivations are more than compensated for by the pleasures appropriate to the natural animal. Biker cynics are likely to take a dim view of convention as surely as convention takes a dim view of them, but where the cynical biker is willing to leave convention to the conventional people, the conventional people seem often to want to judge the cynical biker and tell him how to live. This is where the dominant culture and the "counterculture" (if such it can be called) come toe to toe. The ordinary sense of the term "cynic," a person who takes a contrarian view towards any constructive suggestion with no higher purpose in mind, does apply fairly well to the way the nature's child sees the conventional values that the self-anointed "decent people" like to crow about. But a healthy distaste for the hypocrisy of these suburban roosters is not the same thing as nihilism. Where the people of the suburbs like to inhabit the cages of dogma and opinion they made for themselves, it doesn't take a philosopher to recognize that if those people were really comfortable with the values they like to talk about, they wouldn't see it as a challenge when someone else lives by different ones. Those who feel threatened when their way of life fails to be universally embraced by every single person in the world are working on a kind of psychosis that, in its logical end, becomes totalitarian. Happy Jack, in the rare moments when he isn't happy, is quite willing to shock the middle class and then laugh at how easily they are offended. They might say he is a "cynic" in the common sense of that term, and that isn't altogether wrong, but it is such a small part of the story.

It's not easy to know how to explain this to you, but before I do, I want you to understand that there are as many ways to embody the nature's child as there are ways to follow the calls of nature itself. Happy Jack is not the only sort. He is a common variation on a recognizable theme. Jack does not always respect his body, but he thoroughly inhabits it, and *it* is all that *he* is, and he does pretty much with it what he damn well pleases. One thing that pleases him is a powerful bike between his legs. There are two things that he looks for in a bike: the most important of the two is how it feels under him, and the second is how it looks (make no mistake, he wants everyone to look at it, although for fun he may tell *you* not to look). He chooses his women the same way, and the women *do* like Happy Jack. Jack gets a new bike and a new woman about every two years or so. All his women are just as tricked out as his rides. I am only going to talk about the bikes, but he modifies both in about the same ways. The last one I saw him on started out as an FXSTDI Softail Deuce, 88ci, fuel injected, and built for speed, but you

Stoicism, or the Damaged Biker

Gary is damaged. In his case it came from his tours in Nam, but the details are not so important. Sometimes things happen to good bikers that just can't be set right. Plenty of bad things happened to Cowboy and Bear and Jack, but I think Gary's heart was a little softer, a little more open, maybe he was a little less jaded about life when he went to Nam. He was pretty young— Gary isn't the luckiest guy I've ever known; his lottery number was five. That's pretty much the way it has gone for him ever since. Chance is so much a part of what has happened to him, but he can only see it as fate, and he cannot bring himself to embrace it fully by any effort of heart or mind. He used to tell his stories to anyone who would listen, back before he got sober, but now he is a little more reserved. I wouldn't say he has found *apatheia*, as the stoics call it, that peace of mind that comes from rising above the more violent emotions, but Gary goes one day at a time, some days are better, some are worse.

Natural stoics do not become bikers; natural stoics often become ruthless corporate types or politicians or lawyers or even cops. But sometimes bikers do become stoics. Strong passions are universal among bikers, but time and bad luck can make a biker into a functional sort of stoic. Such bikers are pretty well consumed by their own demons and what they want more than anything else is rest from all the inner turmoil. So the stoicism that we associate with the dominant Hellenistic current of thought is not exactly the same as the stoicism we find in the biker bar. Hellenistic stoicism started around 300 B.C.E. with Zeno of Citium and prospered up through the fourth century C.E. Perhaps its most illustrious voices were Seneca (around 4 B.C.E.–65 C.E.), a minister of Nero and a playwright; Epictetus (50–138 C.E.), a freed slave and bodyguard of Nero, and the Roman Emperor Marcus Aurelius (121–180 C.E.). The appeal of this philosophy was that it saw all events in the universe as being sufficiently caused and fully explained by the laws of nature. The key to human happiness, therefore, was to adjust the human world, both the inner life and the social, political, and economic life to these laws. The laws of nature were the key to knowledge, virtue, prosperity, truth, and happiness. Unhappiness was maladjustment of human things to the very source of justice, which is the cosmos and its law. The cosmos was morally indifferent to human aspirations, but it was possible for human beings to adjust themselves to the way things are, to learn to embrace the inevitable, and to achieve an inward calm about it. Learn to "love your fate," they said, or call it *amor fati* when we get back to the coffee house, if we ever do.

One major difference between natural stoics and bikers who have become stoic is that natural stoics very often see embracing convention as a wise course towards inner calm. Stoic bikers are no more at home within conventional values than they are living beyond them. This is because the stoic biker is not at home with himself. There is a contradiction embedded in the heart of stoicism that the bikers exhibit more obviously than the natural stoics. The contradiction can be phrased in general terms like this: if the cosmos is so all-fired orderly, how can humans ever succeed in being out of adjustment with it? Without turning this issue towards psychoanalysis, one can suspect that the entire stoic philosophy is an act of projected wish fulfillment made desirable by the inescapable disorderliness of the inner life. The difference between the "natural" stoic and the damaged biker is that the natural stoic has so many layers of compensation that he or she has become cut off from that inner life. In short, natural stoics are unfamiliar with their own passions, and have chosen to be, and have safe-guarded their chosen self-ignorance with a veritable Department of Homeland Security that could turn away even the best efforts of Socrates. The damaged biker is unlikely to succeed in being this dishonest with himself and the world. Periodic bouts of decompensation during which the press to self-honesty is too keenly experienced to be ignored can lead to erratic behavior on the part of bikers like Gary.

Gary has done some things he is not proud of. He did some time at Marion, and some at Bellevue, and he has been in and out of the VA's rehab programs many times. There is nothing you can think of that Gary hasn't been addicted to, at one time or another, and he looks a lot older than he is. He has a grown son he has never met, and two other kids in Colorado, but their mother Gina won't let Gary see them. The courts have agreed. Gary is still in love with Gina, but he has given up on getting that back, since she eventually gave up on him. I think she still loves him, too. It is tragic. But for all that, he is a loyal friend. He means well and for the last six or eight years he has done all right. Cowboy and Rose look after him to the extent he needs it, and he looks after them in his own way. Gary is fearless. I remember one night when my band was playing over on that stage, I saw Gary head purposefully over to that far corner in the dark there, and about a minute later, I saw Cowboy head the same way with a baseball bat. I couldn't see what happened on account of the lights, but I found out later that an idiot had pulled a gun and that Gary was standing between that dude and his intended target daring him to pull the trigger when Cowboy broke the dude's arm into tiny pieces. The county sheriff hauled the idiot away. I am happy to say that those sorts of incidents are really pretty rare here, but when you bring this many strong individuals together, sometimes there is trouble.

I mentioned that Gary rides that Shovelhead Cowboy gave him. In his wilder days it wasn't unusual for Gary to go for the drastically modified custom jobs. He worked for a famous customizer in LA for a while. Recently Gary took up with a gal named Patty. She seems to understand him and he treats her well, appreciates her. She has her own baggage. I guess it would be closer to the truth to say that they are genuinely fond of each other than to call it love, since love is too dangerous a passion for either of them at this point. We all hope that Gary has finally found equilibrium, but it is unwise to get invested in that hope. If his luck is better from here on out, Gary might be able to stay sober, but all that depends on keeping his demons quiet, which is the extent of his stoicism.

So What of It?

In a certain sense, it's pointless to try to classify bikers philosophically. If there is one thing they have in common, it is their individualism. But unlike the coffee-house Emersonians who long for an original relation to the universe, the bikers I know find that original relation a pretty easy thing to accomplish. All a fellow has to do is live free and the original relation will take care of itself. The key to living free is knowing who you are, and the path to learning who you are is your own responsibility. Respect the people who respect themselves, guard your own honor, and follow your own *daimon*, the voice that comes in through the back of your mind in the quiet moments, and you can probably learn what you need to know. Another important commonality among all these types of free spirits is an intuitive awareness that happiness is fleeting, uncommon, not to be expected, and always to be celebrated wherever it alights for a time. You might call this pagan fatalism, but I don't see that naming it something so ominous gets you any closer to understanding it, especially since it is really all about freedom. Courage is also indispensable for a life that strives to be free, which involves a willingness to face and accept the consequences of your choices, even the consequences that are yours by bad luck.

With this much said, it might now be safe to say that, predominantly, bikers are pagans (Bikers for Jesus being ex-pagans). But by "pagan" I do not mean heathen, or anti-Christian, or nature-worshippers. Paganism in the sense I intend is something that exists and thrives in high civilization, and it really rests on a willingness to put embodied practice and action ahead of reflection and hypothesizing. These are really postindustrial, postmodern pagans, making of our world whatever remains to them to make of it. It is difficult to look upon what we have done and not be moved to complete silence. And there is a very great silence that surrounds the culture of the postmodern pagans. This silence speaks volumes, however, saying to the whole world of, well, their technical term is *assholes*: "if I fight your wars, I do it for my own honor, not for your gain; if I obey your laws, I do it because I choose them for myself; if I break your laws, I accept my punishment not at your hand but as the consequence of my own decision to live as I chose; and above all, do not ask me to believe your bullshit."

Life on a Harley. It is a kind of philosophical practicalism that refuses to divorce body from spirit. This is an alternative way of taking the Platonic insights, alternative, that is, to Christian Platonism that *does* divorce body and spirit. One of the great advantages of Biker Platonism, in its various forms, is that it employs honor and freedom rather than guilt as its primary spring to moral living. But to what end? Pretty much the same end as Christianity, summed up well in the John Kay's lines "Here and God are gonna make it happen, take the world in a love embrace, fire all of your guns at once and explode into space." Perhaps readers will recall the scene of Jesus's ascension. There is a certain sense of striving to love the world that informs this deep-seated quest for freedom and self-identity.

Plenty of suburbanites or conformists may be able to find this experience of being at home in the world without leaving the comfort of their living rooms, but as Bruce puts it, his love is bigger than a Honda, bigger than a Subaru. For people who have and need Big Love, the Big Bike recommends itself. So, returning to our theme of the previous chapter, we see that Bruce wouldn't ride a Honda not just because it isn't a suicide machine, but because there just isn't enough *love* in it. How can you really *love* a Honda? Does anyone want to die on a Honda? The Honda conserves itself, and those who ride them do not give themselves to the world in a reckless quest to love life and be loved in the midst of it. Hondas bespeak good sense, but Harleys are for people who can understand that he who would save his life must be willing to lose it. That is where the free love is, which is to say, free love isn't free. I suppose Jesus was really the first true pagan, or maybe it was Socrates.

I don't think anyone is going to talk to us at the Iron Post today. That may be just as well. Finish your beer and we can head back towards town. Maybe you will come here again some time on your own, now that you know where the place is.[5]

---

[5] I would like to thank, apart from all the guys I have known who make up Cowboy, Bear, Happy Jack, and Gary, two sociologists who listened to this as it was being written and offered helpful observations, namely Chuck Peek of the University of Florida and Charlie Peek of Texas Tech University. I think Charlie was the sort of dad who probably *took* Chuck to the Harley dealership rather than waiting for Chuck to ask. I also want to thank my novelist friend Richard Lawrence Cohen for his generous reading and observations.

4

What Can Marx and Hegel Tell Us about Social Divisions among Bikers?

JONATHAN GOLDSTEIN

Have you ever pulled up on your Harley to a biker-friendly watering hole, bellied up to the bar, and just as you start quenching your thirst, found yourself engaged in episodes of intense, mildly menacing eye-locking stares with a fellow biker? In this real life version of the childhood game of who blinks first, you offer a nod of recognition which may be acknowledged in return. This subtle initial power struggle is over; you have assumed a subservient position in this social interaction with your newfound drinking buddy.

Such struggles for power or recognition, both subtle and less subtle, and the resulting social tensions among bikers repeat themselves on many different levels in the biker subculture. Consider some other examples: (1) you just finish wrenching and polishing your 1965 Electra Glide and drive one hundred miles to compete in an antique meet only to be showed up by the guy who trailers his machine with a pit and polishing crew in tow to the event. Does that raise your hackles or elicit any resentment? Have you ever attended a swap meet and found yourself cursing the parasitic profiteers responsible for displacing the ubiquitous tables of authentic used and new oldstock Harley parts with parts and accessories made in Taiwan or China, boutique biker leathers, mass-produced tee-shirts, and garish jewelry? How about the boutique-outfitted biker dude who is better dressed than you were on your wedding day? How often has the compulsion to ask him if he owns a Harley or just a tee-shirt overwhelmed you? Have you ever winced with disdain at a biker scantily clad in shorts and sneakers riding a crotch rocket and passing you at ninety miles per hour? I bet you didn't offer a hand gesture of recognition as he passed. You may have preferred an alternative hand signal, but being on your best behavior you refrained. You may also be guilty of snubbing a fellow passing Harley rider just because he is wearing a helmet. Yet, you fought hard for his freedom to choose whether to wear a helmet or not. Does the conspicuous consumption of top-end Harleys and customized machines by Yuppies and movie stars tarnish your cherished image of the Harley-Davidson tradition?

These divisions—between those who uphold traditional Harley culture and those who have redefined it, those who wrench and ride versus those who trailer and ride the last mile, between the rich urban bikers (RUBs) with their spiffy new rides and the working class heroes who mortgage their home to eat, sleep, and drink Harley-Davidson, between helmeted and non-helmeted riders, riceburner riders versus riders of culturally correct machines, and between one-percenters and the rest of us—are but a small subset of evolving divisions between bikers. Given that it takes two to tango, it doesn't matter on which side of these splits you reside. Such divisions can have disturbing consequences for both sides.

Were bikers always so divided? Most old-time bikers would probably tell you no. Prior to the era of mass-marketed motorcycles, the main struggles were between bikers and nonbikers. While these conflicts still exist today with lifestyle-regulating decisions such as helmet laws lying in the balance, bikers have diverted their attention from protecting their lifestyle from outside attacks by turning on themselves. The resulting disharmony has weakened the survival of this subculture.

The evolution of social divisions among bikers and their contradictory consequences should be of interest to any motorcyclist intent on preserving the Harley tradition. I maintain that such an understanding is best discerned with the aid of the conceptual approaches of two nineteenth-century German philosophers: Karl Marx (1818–1893) and Georg Hegel (1770–1831).

Would Marx or Hegel Have Ridden a Harley-Davidson?

For the uninitiated, Karl Marx is usually vilified as the father of communism much as AMF was blamed for the mid-1970s decline of Harley-Davidson. Hegel is a philosopher whose obscurity has grown with time just as stories about leaking, "mark your spot Harleys" have faded from the biker vernacular. Yet, from the perspective of the history of philosophy, Marx and Hegel were seminal thinkers. They were the first great social system modelers who focused on the evolution of human history. Their innovative theories shared a common philosophy: all aspects of society are contradictorily composed of different pushes and pulls resulting in tensions that resolve themselves through ever-changing contradictory social interactions between individuals. These interactions act as the motor of history through their impact on the political, economic, and cultural aspects of society. For both Marx and Hegel, change was understood through the use of an important concept that should be organically understood by Harley riders: the dialectic. Keep in mind that contradiction lies at the heart of the dialectic.

Hegel's Dialectic

Hegel's dialectic was quite simple, while Marx's was more complex. Hegel's dialectic consists of a confrontation between a thesis, its antithesis (opposite), and the resulting working-out of contradictions called the synthesis. Here, synthesis need not imply a compromise or a blending of thesis and antithesis. The outcome could range from a new set of contradictory relations to a new harmonious set of interactions. For example, you and your newfound drinking buddy could resolve any tensions by fighting or going for a long ride together.

While the dialectic sounds like a complex idea, Harley riders have a leg up on grasping this notion because typically their lives are walking contradictions. The social stigma that citizens and the media have attached to the Harley culture underlies the fine contradictory line that many bikers walk between the biker universe and the real world. Yet, having a conflict-ridden life is only halfway to grasping the dialectic. The other half involves becoming conscious of how the contradictory social relations encountered in these two worlds work themselves out and impact not only one's life but also change the different environments in which an individual coexists. Most Harley riders are acutely aware of the conflicts that result from their choice to straddle two cultures. One site of conflict is a Harley rider's work life. Others are marital or cohabitating relations, political interactions, and relations with relatives, the law, and other bikers.

For example, consider the day that I arrived at my new job as a college professor at a conservative liberal-arts college riding my 1958 Pan Head. Never has the contradictory nature of my life choices been so evident. My professional greeting was tepid, to say the least. It was not long before I was derided for my dress, personal appearance, choice of friends, fraternization with students, student field trips to biker bars, and choice of language. Sound familiar? I was acutely aware that my promotion decision would be a political one, rather than one solely based on merit. My research on motorcycle helmet effectiveness, despite its sound basis and technical merits, was not well received. The scheduling of biker research interviews at the same time and place as a campus-hosted regional art festival for tourists and yuppies resulted in further clashes of unyielding interests. As a result, an adversarial relationship between the college administration and me emerged and exists to this very day.

Yet on that same first day, I rode down the hill to town and randomly parked my bike on Main Street. Being in a foreign place, I threaded a lock and chain through the front wheel. Well, it wasn't long before the old Pan and its anchor, as one old timer referred to my unusually large chain, drew a crowd. Upon my return, I was welcomed by a group of local bikers who became an undying support network and an introduction to a rich biker lifestyle in an unfamiliar place. The contradictory pushes and pulls between these two universes acting as if two gravitational forces were colliding and competing can be used to understand my evolution in and between each of these two worlds. If I were to bore you with the details, it would be an application of Hegel's dialectical method and it would explain contradictory outcomes: my earning tenure, battling the college administration on benefit issues, performing interesting helmet research, joining the biker's rights movement, and so forth. Alternatively, we can learn more about the relevance of the dialectic for Harley riders from Marx and Hegel's theories of human history.

How did Hegel apply his dialectic? Hegel embraced the ideals of the French Revolution (liberty, equality, and fraternity). He believed that such a civil society embodied the notion of universal recognition—equitable treatment for all citizens via the eradication of relations of domination and subservience. Hegel believed that the master plan for civil society was developed by God and that God directed the evolution of human history through implanting the Absolute Idea—an innate desire to be recognized—in the mind and will of individuals. This served as the catalyst for contradictory social interactions and resulting social change.

For Hegel, change is the result of the dialectical interaction between individuals engaged in relationships of dominance and subservience. Hegel employs his simple dialectic where a thesis (Absolute Idea or innate desire to be recognized) confronts an antithesis (lack of recognition in a real world situation) and results in a synthesis-change (a change in relations of dominance). For Hegel, change was always uni-directional; a movement closer to universal recognition. Eventually, society evolves to the Prussian state, which Hegel embraced as the realization of universal recognition. Hegel declares that history has ended with the Prussian state—the motor of future change, lack of recognition, had run out of fuel. This conclusion was convenient for Hegel, who was a high-level functionary in the Prussian state eager to preserve his privileged position.

Thus Hegel, a status quo guy, would likely not have ridden a Harley. He would never jeopardize his privileged position by adopting cultural practices outside of the norm. Despite this, Hegel's dialectic is relevant for understanding divisions among bikers. The desire or will to be recognized, whether innate or acquired, in dialectical fashion both attracts and repels bikers of all stripes. Freedom-seeking riders overcome the alienation of restrictive regulation of their lifestyle by uniting, while subsets of bikers are left to struggle with injustices imposed by politically dominant groups within the bikers right movement and more generally by traditional culture purists.

Marx's Dialectic

Marx would likely have embraced Harley culture. In contrast to Hegel, Marx's dialectic was complex. To him, contradiction was multidimensional, moving beyond a simple confrontation between thesis and antithesis. He considered a complexity of social interactions comprising any aspect of society. Returning to my autobiographical example, the Harley rider-professor dichotomy would be extended to include my upbringing in a working-class community, first-generation college graduate status, participation in the civil rights, antiwar, and student rights movements, and other aspects of my life to better understand the complexity and multitude of contradictory pushes and pulls that underlie my behavior.

Marx's approach was inspired by his observation of the disorderly social conflict based on class antagonisms and political coalitions between social classes in the period following the bourgeois-capitalist revolutions in Europe.[1] Where Hegel saw harmony and stability emerging out of the French Revolution, Marx saw chaos and contradiction.

For Marx, the main motor of history was the antagonism among a complex set of social interactions that goes well beyond the stereotypical struggle between workers and capitalists. More specifically, Marx analyzed the intensely competitive process (an interaction between different types of capitalists) in the market economy, and a matrix of interactions between capitalists, laborers, bankers, landowners, foreign capitalists, and a series of institutions. He focused not only on how these interactions affected the distribution of income and its impact on the work, consumption, and investment activities of society's inhabitants, but also on class interests and social activities in the political, economic, and cultural spheres of society. Marx used this analysis to locate contradictory elements of capitalist development such as

---

[1] Marx observed the struggles between the three great classes of the time: fledgling capitalists, the previously powerful landed aristocracy weakened by the transition from feudalism to capitalism, and the growing working class made more populous by the transition from the agricultural countryside to industrial cities. The first half of the nineteenth century was a period of social turmoil that saw the previously powerful landed aristocracy attempt to reassert power/control over the new social system and a growing working class demanding reforms of the new socioeconomic system. Various coalitions between these classes were formed over the period. Ultimately with the defeat of the Revolutions of 1848, the fledgling capitalist class more firmly secured its dominant position.

the occurrence of periodic recessions, unemployment as a norm, poverty and the need for a welfare state, the evolution of large corporations, economic injustice, and a dependency on foreign trade.

The relevance of Marx's dialectic for understanding biker social relations and the resultant threats to the preservation of the Harley culture is that contradictory social relations can be complex and can transcend the place where they originate. Thus, the resolution of economic contradictions, in good dialectical fashion, may have dire contradictory consequences for cultural activities including Harley culture.

Marx was a proponent of the working class, particularly under the injustices and subservience that it experienced under capitalism. As such, he would have been supportive of working-class culture and thus would have analyzed and identified with trends in Harley culture. He was also a radical thinker who liked making a statement. Thus, he may have even ridden a Harley with a flame paint job. Although Marx, who lived a life of near-poverty, probably could not have afforded the admission price.

Enough of the philosophy lesson. You get the basic point: power relations are prevalent and are ever-changing with potential spillover effects from their source to other aspects of life. Let's get back to social divisions among bikers.

The Evolution of Biker Social Relations

Despite the varied socioeconomic backgrounds of bikers, social divisions among bikers were minimal throughout the 1960 to mid-1970s period and most likely during earlier eras.[2] Bikers included World War II and Vietnam vets; they hailed from working-class backgrounds; they were country boys raised on dirt bikes and hill climbers and counterculture enthusiasts keen on experiencing alternative lifestyles. The common thread between these groups was that they were motorcycle enthusiasts, adventurers, and freedom seekers. Bikers during this period formed a brotherhood. Symbolic of this fraternal or co-respective relationship was the way riders greeted each other on the road. The preferred greeting was a clenched fist symbolizing solidarity

---

[2] Although, there had always been a rivalry between Indian and Harley riders.

among riders. In this era, it was less important *what* you rode (Honda 350s and 450s, Kawasaki Avengers and Mach II's, and Italian-made Harley Sprints included), and more pertinent *that* you rode. In Hegelian terms, this situation was a form of universal recognition and freedom (of the road), but unlike Hegel's idealized world of everlasting mutual respect, this one would be short-lived.

Biker social relations soon changed from being fraternal to involving fraternal rivalry. This change mirrors a transition in the competitive environment between motorcycle manufactures (a social interaction that Marx would have analyzed) from fraternal/co-respective competition to fratricidal competition. Prior to 1970, motorcycle producers were primarily enthusiasts and riders producing machines for a limited market of like-minded enthusiasts. Despite the large number of companies during the first few decades of motorcycle production, the limited demand, and the eventual demise of all U.S. manufactures with the exception of Harley-Davidson, competition between manufacturers was restrained. Price competition was limited and competitive advances were primarily made through successes on the track, winning of war contracts, branding, model development, and advertising.

This early competitive phase is replaced by intense price competition initiated by Japanese manufactures exploiting advanced technology to produce new models that directly competed with the larger displacement machines produced by Harley and others. Additionally, the Japanese firms were adept at mass marketing their rides, thus overcoming earlier limits to demand[3] (for example, "You meet the nicest people on a Honda"). The mass marketing of the motorcycle occurred in two phases: the Japanese invasion of Harley territory in the 1969–1985 period and the revival and riding of the demographic wave by Harley-Davidson after 1985.

In this first phase, the commodification of the motorcycle takes place. No longer are motorcycles for enthusiasts and adventurers, they become simple commodities for purchase by

---

[3] This process was aided by the first oil crisis and environmental regulations that forced Japanese manufactures to switch to the production of more desirable four-stroke models.

anyone irrespective of their skill, training, or adventurous spirit. As I will argue below, the commodification of the motorcycle leads to major divisions among bikers. Yet, the dominant role of the commodity in market economies can easily lead a casual observer to overlook such divisions. After all, if motorcycles are a common commodity, we are all bikers now. A false sense of biker unity could be perceived. Marx issued a methodological warning about how surface perceptions concerning market activities could be misleading with respect to discerning key social interactions, which he called *commodity fetishism*. Here, a fetish is not the coddling of your Harley through excessive polishing till the chrome wears thin, nor is it the use of handlebars, foot pegs, sissy bars, and the like for unnatural acts. It refers to the misperception that market relations between buyers and sellers are the be all and end all of social interactions in capitalism. There are more important under-the-surface social interactions useful for understanding, in our case, cultural developments.

As first recognized by Marx, the competitive process, a key social interaction, is a dialectical one with both desirable and unwanted economic effects and potentially contradictory spillover effects to other aspects of society. It can be argued that the competitive onslaught against Harley-Davidson, while improving the quality of bikes, directly attacked Harley culture at its core. Of course, as commodity fetishism suggests, the linkage is not a direct one, but this does not imply it is not a crucial one.

The first phase of mass marketing brought a diverse group of riders to motorcycling with dramatically different motivations and with far less commitment to the survival of the sport. Many of the road brands potentially sounded the competitive death knell of Harley-Davidson. This threat was exacerbated by Harley-Davidson's failed strategic response to the competition.[4] As a result of the Japanese invasion and Harley's response, the Harley culture was threatened and a significant split between motorcyclists occurred. The clenched fist, symbolic of a united

---

[4] Harley fell into the hands of a bowling pin manufacturer in order to provide the corporate clout necessary to compete internationally. AMF marketed and packaged Harleys in an innovative way, but at the same time its inability to maintain and improve quality undermined its strategy and threatened the survival of the brand.

brotherhood, gave way to the more traditional hand wave brought along from the nonmotorcycling experiences of new riders. As resentment mounted, the hand wave was replaced by the selective hand wave or snub. A once tight brotherhood was divided.

At the same time, civil society became less civil. Liberal elements decided that it was necessary to protect other elements from themselves. Universal recognition became selective, particularly in the form of mandatory helmet use legislation. The response was the formation of biker rights organizations. Their origin is directly associated with the core Harley culture. In dialectical fashion, this movement was aided by the very forces that threatened to make such groups fail, the commodification of the motorcycle. As bikes became ordinary household items, their perception as the toys or weapons of hard-core deviants was softened, but not by enough to stem the tide of states adopting helmet laws. The ultimate solution required a representative membership in biker rights groups and thus some uneasy alliances between originators and mass-market riders. This typically takes the form of open membership and open events, but tight control of decision-making by core enthusiasts. This scenario reproduced tensions between the groups, but also maintained some equilibrium. Symbolic of these biker social relations is the change in the translation of the ABATE acronym to a more palatable form from All Brothers Against Totalitarian Enactments to American Bikers Aimed Toward Education.

The second phase of the competitive process and mass marketing, characterized by a mid-course correction made by Harley-Davidson in time to exploit the baby boomers' spending of discretionary income, also changed the course of biker social relations. The Willie G. era of improved quality and more highly stylized machines, many with nostalgic themes, successfully tapped this ready source of leisure consumption funds. This phase added two more groups of bikers to the mix: yuppies and working-class stiffs who missed out on the early years of the Harley revolution because they could not afford to pay the price of admission. While the late working-class bloomers have more readily assimilated into the core Harley culture, the yuppie-RUB boomers have had a rougher ride. Their leisure-class mentality deeply divides them from core Harley riders.

Competition is a dynamic process. The newfound popularity of Harley-Davidson has led to the Japanese copycat cruiser and full dresser models. This trend has created a more sophisticated type of Jap bike rider who, while more palatable to Harley riders, has not been fully accepted. In addition, these faux-Harley riders also have distanced themselves from crotch rocket riders. On balance, it's difficult to say whether bikers are more or less unified as a result of this copycat phenomenon.

An additional element of the Harley-Davidson strategy was to market authorized clothing and accessories. This competitive response not only brands the company, but acts as an additional source of revenue. The success of this sideline has resulted in a Harley fashion trend which is antithetical to original Harley culture. In addition, it has spawned alternative profiteers merchandising knockoffs and generic biker accessories. The success of Harley-Davidson's marketing campaign has further divided the biking community into well-coiffed bikers and traditionally dressed riders and has created a class of parasitic profiteers that has invaded swap meets and other events at the expense of more traditional activities. Furthermore the pop-culture status of the brand has generated a class of wannabes who have both embraced and diluted the culture, creating antagonisms between established culture and pop-culture practitioners.

The extension of the traditional culture to include the pop culture has set off the Hegelian desire to be recognized. Pop culturists vie for recognition and gain some acceptance through the biker-rights movement and auxiliary groups affiliated with motorcycle clubs. Despite these superficial acknowledgements, these groups remain second-class citizens in the class structure of the culture. The end result is another source of both support and tension within the ranks of the biker world.

Finally, we can never forget that at the core of the dominant biker culture is the autonomous individual. The biker culture was founded by and for free-willed individuals seeking freedom and adventure. Yet, this autonomous foundation, while uniting bikers, also tears them apart. Hegel's free-willed individuals will pursue positions of dominance and to that end create a class of subservient riders. The playing-out of this dialectic at the level of individual bikers is another source of division and may be the most difficult to overcome. Thus, the fledging relationship between our biker buddies at the bar may never get beyond the individualistic desires to be free, and this may be the biggest obstacle to preserving a culture through biker unity.

Are We All Divided Bikers Now?

The dialectic in its Hegelian and Marxian forms tells us that activities are contradictorily composed of competing and possibly opposite forces. In addition, Marx's concept of commodity fetishism implies that some things may not be what they appear to be on the surface. Using these concepts, we have examined evolving social divisions between bikers. My analysis reveals that within the seeds of these divisions are the seeds of unity and that the primary source of these divisions is not deep-seated differences between riders, but rather is the result of the unfolding of other social interactions, particularly the competition between motorcycle manufactures in the economic sphere. Motorcycle riders are caught up in a whirlwind of competitive forces beyond their control. These tendencies have created divisions far deeper than justified because bikers have incorrectly interpreted differences on a personal level rather than on a societal or economic level. Thus animosities are disproportionate to their basis.

This same analysis makes it evident that Harley riders cannot rely on the Harley-Davidson Motor Co. to preserve the traditional Harley culture. When the company was entrusted with that task in the past, it barely survived, and when it did succeed, it ultimately weakened the culture's own foundation making it teeter on implosion through the creation of further divisions. As Marx would clearly tell us, the main task of Harley-Davidson is to make profits so that it can defend itself against future competitive onslaughts. This objective is not necessarily constrained by the preservation of the core Harley culture.

The best chance for the survival of Harley culture lies within its boundaries. Until bikers recognize that the sources of their differences are shallow and that the commonalities between them are of a higher order of magnitude, they will continue to be sitting ducks for external and internal forces that will conquer their subculture.

While Hegel's free-willed individuals will always remain an obstacle in either a divided or united biker world, the containment of such autonomous individual tendencies through peer pressure is a small price to pay for survival.[5]

---

[5] The author is grateful to Michael S. Morris and Ernie Canelli for many years of shared hard-driven miles and for helpful comments on earlier drafts of this chapter.

SECOND LEG:
200 Miles

The form of things that come into being from human skill is in the soul of the producer.

—ARISTOTLE (*Metaphysics*, Book VII, Chapter 7, 1032b, 1)

The Solomon R. Guggenheim Museum, New York, NY.

5

What Are a Bunch of Motorcycles Doing in an Art Museum?

BERNARD E. ROLLIN

In June of 1988, the Solomon R. Guggenheim museum in New York, one of the world's most prestigious art museums, opened an exhibition entitled "The Art of the Motorcycle," wherein the history of the evolution of the motorcycle was chronicled through more than 130 examples. The exhibition was the best-attended installation in the history of the museum, and also broke attendance records at the Guggenheim museum in Bilbao, Spain.

An obvious question arises concerning both the exhibition and its unparalleled success. In what sense can motorcycles be viewed as works of art? The introduction to the exhibit begins as follows:

> Perhaps more than any other single object of industrial design, the motorcycle can be considered a metaphor for the 20th century. Predating the automobile by 25 years and the airplane by 36, the motorcycle was the first form of personal mechanized transport to emerge from the beginning of the industrial age; its subsequent evolution follows the main currents of modernity.[1]

This statement certainly justifies an historical exhibition on the motorcycle. But it fails to explain why the motorcycle is to be viewed as art.

---

[1] Guggenheim Museum, Past Exhibitions, *The Art of the Motorcycle* (June 26th—September 20th, 1998, http://www.guggenheim.org/exhibitions/past_ exhibitions/motorcycle/motorcycle.html.

For most of the history of the visual arts and sculpture in the West, these genres were played out on a stage of representation. That is, works of art were undertaken in a representational mode, despite immense variation in what counted as representation.

Simply stated, representational art shows things looking as they appear in the real world, as opposed to abstract art, which isn't concerned with accurately depicting things. Whether what is being depicted is real or fictitious, secular or religious, most of historical fine art recognizably intends to picture some aspect of reality, whether to immortalize, evoke emotion, depict an alternative reality, or simply to chronicle some slice of life. Representational skills, be it in the works of legendary fifth-century B.C. painter Zeuxis, who is said to have painted grapes so realistic that the birds pecked at them, or the expressive agony of face and body captured in Lucas Cranach's crucifixion paintings, or the overtly frightening depictions of the torments of hell by Bosch, play an iconic role in evoking aesthetic response to art.

Indeed it is not until the late nineteenth century that Western art begins to break away from the representational tether, for a variety of reasons. Most plausibly, the invention and refinement of photography in some ways made representation superfluous. Secondarily, new exposure to African, American Indian, and other cultural traditions broke the hold of representation on the artistic and cultural communities. Third, the beginning of the twentieth century brought a reaction against complexity in all areas of culture, epitomized by the Bauhaus School (an early-twentieth-century German school of design) in visual art and architecture, and Arnold Schoenberg (in contradiction to Gustav Mahler and Richard Wagner) in music. The stage was set in various ways for the modernist reaction against representation, and for new theories of art, which would accommodate these artistic changes.

Given the bewildering array of objects that have counted as art since the beginning of the twentieth century—Marcel Duchamp's urinal, Andy Warhol's soup cans, people engaged in self-mutilation—it has been suggested by the philosopher Morris Weitz that art is inherently indefinable, with new art objects grouped under the art rubric sharing at best a series of overlapping resemblances.[2] Art is allegedly an "open concept," and not subject to hard definition. Such a view certainly accounts for why we can include completely new artistic approaches under the old concept. What is wrong with this approach is that many things we don't wish to call art share overlapping "family resemblances" with what we do. Also, this view is not enlightening— it does not at all help our understanding of, for example, why the Guggenheim chose to display motorcycles and not wheelbarrows. So even if the "open concept" view is true, it does not greatly illuminate what we call art and why we do so.

Another approach which seems fruitful and which denies Weitz's claim that art cannot be defined is the view popularly known as the "Institutional Theory," most comprehensively developed by the philosopher George Dickie. On this view, an artifact becomes a work of art when the status of art object is conferred on it by the "artworld," the social institutions in the position sanctioned to determine "artness," in the same way a minister confers marriage or a king knighthood.

> The artworld consists of a bundle of systems: theater, painting, sculpture, literature, music, and so on, each of which furnishes an institutional background for the conferring of the status on objects within its domain. . . . These features of the artworld provide the elasticity whereby creativity of even the most radical sort can be accommodated. A whole new system comparable to the theater, for example, could be added in one fell swoop. What is more likely is that a new subsystem would be added within a system. For example, junk sculpture added within sculpture, happenings added within theater. Such additions might in time develop into full-blown systems. Thus the radical creativity, adventuresomeness, and exuberance of art . . . is possible within the concept of art, even though it is closed by the necessary and sufficient conditions of artifactuality and the conferred status.[3]

This is a very plausible account, and certainly seems to fit the motorcycle case perfectly. The Guggenheim exhibit, and its

---

[2] Morris Weitz, "The Role of Theory in Aesthetics," *Journal of Aesthetics and Art Criticism* (September 1956), pp. 27–35.

[3] George Dickie, from *Art and the Aesthetic* (Ithaca: Cornell University Press, 1974), in Melvin Rader, ed., *A Modern Book of Esthetics*, fifth edition (New York: Holt, Rinehart and Winston, 1979), pp. 459–472.

catalogue, Dickie would say, conferred the status of art upon motorcycles.

This approach has been lampooned by social critic Tom Wolfe in a witty volume called *The Painted Word*,[4] published in 1975, wherein he accuses critics of creating what counts as art in writings of demonstrable silliness. Nonetheless, Wolfe's criticism actually buttresses Dickie's thesis; for however absurd the critics get, they do determine what gets exhibited and sold for big money as art.

While Dickie's thesis helps us understand *how* motorcycles can become art, it does not help us understand *why* motorcycles were so chosen, and why the exhibit touched so many people. If the Guggenheim were to have devoted an exhibit to potato peelers, people would simply not have lined up in droves. In any event, we know from ordinary experience that ordinary people see motorcycles—particularly Harleys—as aesthetic objects. One popular picture book of Harleys is subtitled *Rolling Sculpture*,[5] and any Harley owner can tell stories of groups of people admiringly surrounding the motorcycle and extolling its beauty. My own mother, who saw motorcycles as death traps, and professed no interest in them, would actually address bikers with phrases like "What a beautiful machine!" In other words, many motorcycles evoke an aesthetic response from people, and are considered "beautiful." And since they are man-made artifacts, we can surmise that most people would have no problems seeing them as "works of art" in both the descriptive and evaluative sense of that phrase. The question before us, then, is what is it about at least some motorcycles that evoke such a positive aesthetic response? As I shall argue, there is no single aesthetic theory that explains this, but a variety of approaches provide some explanation when taken collectively.

To be sure, it should not surprise us that one aesthetic theory does not cover the range of objects created in the twentieth century that produce an aesthetic response in us. Even in painting, the diversity of approaches, from abstract expressionism to magic realism to cubism to surrealism, militates against one simple explanation of our aesthetic reaction. If one then includes

---

[4] Tom Wolfe, *The Painted Word* (New York: Farrar, Straus and Giroux, 1975).
[5] Doug Mitchel, *Harley Davidson: Rolling Sculpture* (New York: Barnes and Noble Books, 1999).

the ball bearing exhibited at the Museum of Modern Art, the seemingly random array of "found objects" pioneered by Kurt Schwitters, and the draped acreages created by Christo as art objects, one despairs even more of a single theoretical explanation of the reaction they elicit. In an era where originality and creativity are encouraged, rather than predictability in style, content, and form, a multiplicity of insights are needed to help interpret our reactions to variegated works of art. And, fortunately, modernism and postmodernism sparked the invention of numerous aesthetic theories that, to varying degrees, help us understand.

Some initial light on our task is shed by the final paragraph of the introduction to the exhibition stated earlier:

> The motorcycle is an immortal cultural icon that changes with the times. More than speed, it embodies the abstract themes of rebellion, progress, freedom, sex, and danger. The limits imposed by its possible forms and functions, and the breadth of variation that has been expressed within these limitations, provide a framework in which to examine the motorcycle both as object and as emblem of our century.[6]

One can argue, as does an essay in the catalogue to the exhibition, that the essence of modern culture is speed. Thomas Krens affirms in the essay serving as a preface to the Guggenheim catalogue, "The pursuit of speed can be seen as a primary factor in the advance of singularly twentieth-century technologies from the measures of light, sound, and particles to the development of military weapons and the nature of warfare to the transformation of our concept of distance."[7] The rate at which humans could travel was relatively fixed from antiquity until the advent of engines; the speed of a fast horse, or roughly forty miles per hour. The motorcycle was going considerably faster—over sixty m.p.h.—by the first decade of the twentieth century and, in 1907, Glenn Curtiss, riding an experimental V-8 motorcycle, set the world land speed record at an astounding 136 miles per hour. By the 1920s, commercially produced bikes were guaranteed to

---

[6] Guggenheim Museum, Past Exhibitions.
[7] Thomas Krens, Preface to *The Art of the Motorcycle* (New York: Guggenheim Museum, 1999), p. 6.

exceed one hundred miles per hour. Today, the motorcycle speed record is owned by Harley-Davidson, over 320 miles per hour.

Vehicles that could achieve high speeds gave people a sense of possibilities never imagined; the ability to travel far in brief periods, and the ability to do so totally on one's own (unlike the speed achieved by a locomotive), and with one's own life more or less in one's own hands. And though there are indeed vehicles that go faster than motorcycles absolutely, from an experiential, phenomenological living of speed, nothing feels faster. A jet plane traveling at 500 miles per hour does not at all give us a sense of speed, we rarely even spill our drinks, and often fall asleep. No one falls asleep on a motorcycle. Twenty miles an hour on a moto-cross trail is enough to take the breath away from a novice rider. Despite my now having logged a quarter of a million miles on a motorcycle, I vividly recall my own first ride on the back of a Triumph Bonneville, rocketing from 0 to 60 in a few seconds, feeling like I was sliding off and flying, out of control, an odd amalgam of exhilaration and fear.

Then too, on a motorcycle you are part of the world through which you speed, the wind in your face and hair, the bugs in your mouth and beard remind you constantly that *you* are speeding through the world, rather than, as in an equally fast auto, a machine with you in it. No wonder then, in my experience, that American Indians, whose civilization flourished on fast horseback, revere Harley-Davidsons as "iron horses" and wear T-shirts (as do many bikers) showing a motorcyclist in tandem with a ghostly Indian warrior with the logo "brothers in the wind." Though few reservation Indians can afford a Harley, the shirts are actually ubiquitous on the vast Navajo reservation.

I recall being approached in Albuquerque by two plainly alcoholic Indians. This is common in the Southwest, as they are usually hustling a few bucks from strangers, particularly from bikers, who they see as "bros." These two however, were after something else. They told me that they had just been released from prison after a number of years. "Would you just start the Harley up so we can hear it, please?" they asked. "It helps us realize that we are free." Motorcycles, unlike much faster cars (what bikers call "cages") are archetypal symbols of freedom, and of the danger the freedom brings, and make one savor life.

In the early 1900s, a school of Italian artists known as Futurists captured the essence of modernism as speed obtained through the machine. Embracing violence, speed, and machines as symbols of the future, and condemning traditional art and museums as passé and "cemeteries," the Futurists were drawn to war and Fascism and above all to motion as destroying middle-class comfortable torpor. The most successful Futurist art freezes motion with astounding success—Umberto Boccherini's bronze sculpture *Unique Forms of Continuity in Space* or Gino Severini's painting *Armored Train in Action* could not be more suggestive of movement if they moved; Futurist music froze the sounds of industry and motion. Though often deploying trains and racing cars as symbols, their ideology applies equally well to the motorcycle, for its looks, function, and sound (= music).

The first *Futurist Manifesto,* written in 1909 by Marinetti, could well have been written for the Guggenheim exhibit, and as an aesthetic guide to the motorcycle experience. Indeed the *Manifesto* begins with the following declaration:

> We suddenly heard the famished roar of automobiles [= engines]. Friends, away! Let's go! Mythology and the Mystic ideal are defeated at last [i.e. the historically sanctified Platonic reality]! We're about to see the centaur's birth![8]

(The centaur is a recurrent symbol for the motorcycle.)

And the eleven elements of the *Manifesto* read as follows:

> We intend to sing the love of danger, the habit of energy and fear-lessness.

> 1. Courage, audacity, and revolt will be essential elements of our poetry.
> 2. Up to now literature has exalted a pensive immobility, ecstasy, and sleep. We intend to exalt aggressive action, a feverish insomnia, the racer's stride, the mortal leap, the punch and the slap.
> 3. We affirm that the word's magnificence has been enriched by a new beauty: the beauty of speed. A racing car whose hood is

---

[8] F.T. Marinetti, *The Futurist Manifesto* (1909), widely available online; one source is *Futurism and the Futurists,* "The Founding and Manifesto of Futurism," http://www.futurism.org.uk/manifestos/manifesto01.htm.

adorned with great pipes, like serpents of explosive breath—a roaring car that seems to ride on grapeshot is more beautiful than the *Victory of Samothrace.*

4. We want to hymn the man at the wheel, who hurls the lance of his spirit across the Earth, along the circle of its orbit.

5. The poet must spend himself with ardor, splendor, and generosity, to swell the enthusiastic fervor of the primordial elements.

6. Except in struggle, there is no more beauty. No work without an aggressive character can be a masterpiece. Poetry must be conceived as a violent attack on unknown forces, to reduce and prostrate them before man.

7. We stand on the last promontory of the centuries! . . . Why should we look back, when what we want is to break down the mysterious doors of the Impossible? Time and Space died yesterday. We already live in the absolute, because we have created eternal, omnipresent speed.

8. We will glorify war—the world's only hygiene—militarism, patriotism, the destructive gesture of freedom-bringers, beautiful ideas worth dying for, and scorn for woman. [Recall that the Hell's Angels offered their services in Vietnam.]

9. We will destroy the museums, libraries, academies of every kind, will fight moralism, feminism, every opportunistic or utilitarian cowardice. [Bikers are known for contempt of feminism. Compare the famous T-shirt, " If you can read this, the bitch fell off."]

10. We will sing of great crowds excited by work, by pleasure, and by riot; we will sing the multicolored, polyphonic tides of revolution in the modern capitals; we will sing the vibrant nightly fervor of arsenals and shipyards blazing with violent electric moons; greedy railway stations that devour smoke-plumed serpents; factories hung on clouds by the crooked lines of their smoke; bridges that stride the rivers like giant gymnasts, flashing in the sun with a glitter of knives; adventurous steamers that sniff the horizon; deep-chested locomotives whose wheels paw the tracks like the hooves of enormous steel horses bridled by tubing; and the sleek flight of plans whose propellers chatter in the wind like banners and seem to cheer like an enthusiastic crowd.[9]

---

[9] *Ibid.*

Though decidedly not politically correct and even somewhat ugly, what the Futurists extol does capture some elements of the biker experience—the dimension of the outlaw that Americans are decidedly warm towards (such as Jesse James, Billy the Kid, gangsters in popular culture), the anarchist and rebel, the fighter and warrior. The symbols worn on shirts and skin by outlaw bikers or outlaw wannabe Harley riders—skulls, Vikings, SS runes, iron crosses, werewolves, pirates, even swastikas—extol rebellious outsiders (though, in my experience, these are largely not pro-Nazi political symbols, but rather symbols of rebellion aimed at shocking and engendering unease and even fear). In a world ever increasingly erosive of personal freedom and even of free speech, these symbols stir a sympathetic chord even in people who do not wear them. Unquestionably, then, the Futurist aesthetic captures a number of elements of the biker phenomenon, and helps explain the exhibition.

But there is more to the motorcycle experience than this, and many motorcycles are not symbols of rebellion and non-conformity.

For another perspective on the aesthetic of motorcycles not related to the rebel, but equally explanatory as to the aesthetics of motorcycles, we can turn to the aesthetic theory of John Dewey, as developed in his *Art as Experience* early in the twentieth century.[10] For Dewey, art replicates and attempts to create in people a special feature of ordinary life; having *an experience*, a consummatory passage of time having a beginning, a middle, and an end that can clearly be identified. Such experiences occur all the time as little jewels in one's life, in the most mundane of contexts. Imagine, for example, waking up at dawn after a heavy snowfall in the country, seeing the snow glistening on your driveway, putting on a coat, finding the snow shovel, getting into a rhythm shoveling as you warm up, and finally ending up with a clean driveway, a satisfying glow in your muscles, and a sense of accomplishment. This would exemplify an experience in Dewey's honorific sense, and can occur at any time pretty much in all aspects of life. Artworks are codifications of such experiences, capable of evoking in those who appreciate them an experience. Matter and form combine

---

[10] John Dewey, *Art as Experience* (New York: Minton, Balch and Co., 1934).

to produce an object capable of creating such an experience, and requires both the artist and audience, though at different moments in time. Thus art is continuous with life, and Dewey condemns repetitive jobs where workers gain no aesthetic satisfaction from what they do.

A motorcycle is an endless source of experiences in Dewey's sense. Consider a very mundane task such as driving to work. You enter the garage, pull out the car, and are barely conscious of the drive, thinking instead about trivial or major problems. Not so on a cycle—as one rider said to me, "It makes magic out of going to work." With a 360-degree view of the sunrise, the sound of the engine, the never-ending thrill of initial acceleration, the waves and thumbs-up from other bikers and cars, and the need to be totally aware, to avoid the semi-zombie state of a car driver, to watch for gravel and oil and other vehicles, the thrill of morning cold piercing your clothing, the changes in temperature as you move from green fields to city streets, each ride is a potential experience in Dewey's sense.

Since my son was eight, for eighteen years he and I have taken a two-week motorcycle summer trip through the American West, Montana to New Mexico, Nebraska to Nevada. Unlike other vacations and trips we have taken, which are vague in our minds, every bike trip remains as a Deweyan experience made up of smaller Deweyan experiences—the time we drove into the Jemez reservation and watched construction workers build a Kiva, and sprinkle us with their hose to mitigate the 100-degree heat, and giggle as we spun around, angry, and then laughed together. The time my engine blew when my son was nine in the middle of nowhere at twilight and his unspoken fear: "What will we do, Daddy?" And we were picked up by the driver of a ranch truck who tied the bike down and found us a motel, in a little town where all the restaurants were closed, but we bought canned spaghetti and bologna and chocolate chip cookies and white bread and milk to create a splendid feast. And our joy the next day when my friend brought his truck to rescue us. And the Navajo police chief on a Harley, who stopped us to tell us that a helmet was required on the reservation and as our faces fell, he added, "You'll note I'm not wearing one! Have a good day." And the envious looks of children trapped in station wagons cast at my son, who swelled up with pride. And the time the starter went out 300 miles from a shop and my eleven-year-old had to push his 250-pound father on the 700-pound bike with a hundred pounds of luggage to a start each time we stopped, with people yelling, "That's child abuse, Mister."

To look at a bike in a museum is to live these experiences again for those who ride. And for those who do not, the beauty of the machine foreshadows such experiences, and the experience of freedom and speed and infinite possibilities offered to the rider. "Some day I'll have one of those" is the aesthetic reaction of nonriders to all motorcycles, but particularly to Harleys. People feel, briefly at least, how their lives could be transmuted, how they could soar above the mundane into a mode of being replete with Deweyan experiences.

I wish I had a dollar for every time, riding alone, burned brown by the sun, clad in the black, weary yet quintessentially alive, I have been approached by women of all ages, who say, "I've always wanted to ride one of those, could you give me a ride?" And when I say "sure," they back away, afraid that a fantasy realized is a disappointment, content to appreciate from outside, yearning for the speed, sound, wind and risk from a safe distance. My wife has talked of buying me a little flag to wave, which says, "I'm not your fantasy object, I'm just a philosophy teacher."

A final aesthetic-theoretical approach to understanding the lure of the motorcycle grows out of the Bauhaus revolution against the ornate and ultimately degenerate excesses of *fin-de-siècle* art—the froufrou art that prevailed at the end of the 1800s. For the Bauhaus, form should follow function; hence elephant feet umbrella stands and lamps fashioned of nymphs and satyrs cavorting on bronze rocks with landscape-looking shades were monstrosities. The founder of the Bauhaus school, Walter Gropius, aimed at obliterating established distinctions between fine art, crafts, and industry. Under the influence of Bauhaus principles, the Museum of Modern Art would exhibit polished ball bearings or airplane propellers as objects of art whose beauty consists in their perfect adaptation to their function.

Motorcycles and their components are paradigmatic examples of design where form follows function. A motorcycle at rest suggests the possibility of fast movement, and of power, and of new Deweyan experiences. There are few extraneous decorative fillips on any motorcycles, and they are, aesthetically, what they do. And in the only purely aesthetic aspect of a motorcycle, the paint jobs, we experience the free play of fine art, from the inherent beauty of primary colors like fire-engine red gleaming from paint jobs that look permanently wet, to airbrushed renditions of abstract designs, to meticulously rendered skeleton figures of the four Horsemen of the Apocalypse or surrealist landscapes. In the end, motorcycles are Bauhausian sculptures that do what they look like with room for infinite modification expressing the rider's individual aesthetic.

Any motorcycle—but particularly Harleys—which are, in a sense, the Platonic form of a motorcycle emulated and plagiarized by others, is a piece of industrialized sculpture, as elegantly at home in a gallery or store window as it is burning up the roads. And in addition to its functional nature, a motorcycle is an investment in a work of art. What other object can be used for years as it is meant to function, and yet not only keep its financial value but actually grow in value? My own Harley has ninety thousand miles; I purchased it for six thousand dollars and could now sell it for twelve thousand. Although mass-produced vehicles, Harleys are almost never left as they came from the assembly line, but are customized by individual riders to reflect their own aesthetic. A bike bought for $25,000 from a dealer may immediately be majorly rebuilt for an additional $10,000 or $20,000 more, with the aim of turning it into one's unique aesthetic creation. This is truly an example of how high technology and mass production can make each individual an artist, creating a work that, like fine art, will usually appreciate in value.

Finally, motorcycles have ever-increasingly diverged from cars. Cars have become increasingly automated, replete with cruise control, navigator computers that talk to the driver, and electronic parts that take the "I" out of driving. There are those who project a future automobile that does not require a driver, where the machine is centrally controlled and the would-be driver becomes a passenger. Such changes are not seriously projected for motorcycles, for motorcyclists largely do not ride for practical reasons, despite those who extol their mileage per gallon; many cars get better mileage than some bikes. Motorcyclists ride largely for the aesthetic experiences riding provides, from being nearly out of control or extending total concentration not to get killed, from getting soaked in warm summer rain to being totally dry an hour later. In a deepest sense, riding takes skill that driving a car does not, skill that one can take pride in, much as we once took pride in horsemanship.

Finally, whereas death and danger were constant companions for our ancestors, be it from infection, highwaymen, wild animals, or enemies, Western society has sanitized our lives. On a motorcycle, in Heidegger's immortal phrase, we come face to face on a regular basis with "the possibility of the impossibility of one's being," the prospect of death. Whether this serves, as in Heidegger's philosophy, as a call to authenticity in one's life choices and decisions, or merely, like hot sauce, enhances the experience of ordinary life, it unquestionably creates a profound aesthetic experience which in and of itself licenses a motorcycle to be considered a fountain of aesthetic experience and thence a work of art.

As philosopher Gilles Deleuze remarks in *Proust and Signs*, "The modern work of art is a machine and functions as such. . . . Why a machine? Because the work of art, so understood, is essentially productive—productive of certain truths."[11]

---

[11] Gilles Deleuze, *Proust and Signs* (Minneapolis: University of Minnesota Press, 2000), p. 149.

6

Motorcycling, Nihilism, and the Price of Cool

ALAN R. PRATT

Raw, loud, and dangerous,[1] the choice of thrill seekers and adrenaline junkies for a hundred years, the motorcycle's powerful juju has made it a colossal icon of popular culture, symbolizing values associated with freedom, rebellion, and, in the latter half of the twentieth century, a nihilistic Fuck the World (FTW) attitude.

Early in the 1960s, the motorcycle and rebellion came together in an unusual way with the emergence of the outlaw biker lifestyle. What's fascinating is how in the last twenty years the trappings of outlaw biker culture have been co-opted, cleaned-up, and commercialized for mass consumption, making the outlaw biker the dominant fashion model for the motorcycle industry.

The sanitized image of the outlaw biker is now the stuff of romantic fantasy, conjuring up images of Vikings, pirates, and desperados. These now-trendy rebels celebrated for their iconoclasm are "as American as apple pie," a documentary points out, "direct descendants of Billy the Kid, Jesse James, and other freedom-loving spirits of the untamed frontier."[2]

---

[1] And, according to Sigmund Freud, supremely phallic. In *The Interpretation of Dreams* (New York: Avon Books, 1965), Freud wrote, "It is highly probable that all complicated machinery and apparatus occurring in dreams stand for the genitals (and as a rule male ones)" (p. 391). *Straddling* loud, complicated machinery like a motorcycle, then, has unmistakable phallic authority—no other machine comes close. This could be one source of the motorcycle's symbolic power and almost mystical adoration.

[2] *The Wild Ride of the Outlaw Biker: Real and Imagined.* Video. Peter Jones Productions, 1999.

Before the outlaw biker style became cool, however, outlaw bikers were feared and loathed by the public. Getting plenty of sensationalized attention from the media, they were most often associated with unseemly acts of drunkenness, irresponsibility, and gratuitous violence, and their chopped scoots had less to do with cool than mayhem. True, these rebels smashed icons, but what the public noticed was that they smashed skulls, too. Besides the notions of freedom, brotherhood, and machismo, then, there was a more powerful underlying theme to the out-biker lifestyle—*nihilism.*

Nihilism—*Danger of Dangers*

In the latter half of the nineteenth century, Friedrich Nietzsche (1844–1900) pointed out that all we really know about life is that it's uncertain, unjust, and cruel. Our highest principles, our knowledge, and our claims to the absolute are nothing more than hopeful interpretations, all of which, the philosopher noted, are false. *Nothing is true.* This insight is the beginning of nihilism—*"the danger of dangers,"* as Nietzsche called it.[3] A nihilist understands that all knowledge is perspectival, that no position is better than another, that there is no measure for good and evil, and that nothing has inherent value, including life itself. A true nihilist, then, repudiates all values, believes in nothing, has no loyalties and no purpose other than, perhaps, an impulse to destroy. It's an epiphany that releases tremendous annihilating forces.

Nietzsche was convinced that the powerful corrosive effects of nihilism would undermine and eventually destroy all moral, religious, and metaphysical convictions and precipitate the greatest catastrophe in history (p. 3). As he predicted, Western culture in the twentieth century—"The Age of Anxiety"—was permeated with nihilism. The most influential philosophical movement of the century, Existentialism, for example, focused on solving the problems posed by the loss of cosmic meaning.

For the French existentialist Albert Camus (1913–1960), nihilism was the most vexing problem of the century. It reveals that life is not a pilgrimage, a program, or a goal; instead, it's a

---

[3] Friedrich Nietzsche, *The Will to Power* (New York: Vintage, 1967), p. 45.

very unpleasant event. We're marooned in an indifferent universe where our frantic efforts to discover meaning come to nothing. Appropriately, Camus chose Sisyphus as a metaphor for the absurdity of the human condition. The mythical figure was condemned to push a huge boulder up a hill, only to have it roll to the bottom again and again *forever.* "The workman of today works every day in his life at the same tasks," Camus wrote, "and this fate is no less absurd."[4]

What's to be done, then? Camus identified two options for coming to terms with meaninglessness—suicide or rebellion. Those who don't have the stomach to face the futility of existence escape the problem with a kind of intellectual suicide, embracing "some stupid little fanaticism," as Nietzsche put it, and allowing others to choose meaning for them. The better option, Camus proposed, is to rebel against the meaninglessness of life: "There is no fate that cannot be surmounted by scorn" (p. 91). Sneering at the indifference of the universe—*by giving it the finger*—only this will permit a modicum of dignity. The existential rebel understands this: life is not a goal; it's an *attitude.* The benefit: Living in a state of rebellion against an absurd existence destroys guilt and allows the rebel to experience total freedom.

The danger, though, is that total freedom can be used in very nasty ways. As a solution to the problem of absurdity, one can justifiably lash out at the world and everyone in it because with nihilism, *any* goal or value is equally worthy or unworthy—universal happiness or universal annihilation. Take your pick. As the impact of nihilism spread and with it the destruction of values, Camus anticipated phenomena like the Fuck the World style. In his philosophical essay *The Rebel* (1951), for instance, he describes how metaphysical collapse often ends in total negation and the victory of nihilism. In such instances, rebellion is characterized by profound hatred, pathological destruction, incalculable violence, and death.

American responses to nihilism are unique in that they tend to be self-indulgent and narcissistic. And whether or not the masses are able to name the phenomenon, it's clear that nihilism

---

[4] Albert Camus, *The Myth of Sisyphus and Other Essays* (New York: Knopf, 1955), p. 90.

troubles the public psyche. The Beats, Pop Art, Hippies, Goths, television culture, spectator sports, Punk Rock, Death Metal, and New Ageism can all be understood as responses to nihilism. And the pervasiveness of Postmodernism, which embraces the notion that all truths and all beliefs are of equal value, is yet another symptom of nihilism's caustic effect. The most fascinating example of nihilism in American popular culture, however, is associated with the motorcycle.

"What Are You Rebelling Against?" "Whad' Ya Got?"

The motorcycle's association with nihilism probably began in 1947 when four thousand drunken savages, "straight pipers," wreaked havoc in Hollister, California—or so it was reported. Motorcycling would never be the same.

Hollywood cashed in on motorcycle-themed nihilism with its version of events in Hollister in László Benedek's *The Wild One* (1954), the granddaddy of all biker films. Marlon Brando's Johnny, a brooding, surly, self-destructive punk in black leather, would prove iconic. While his Black Rebel gang terrorizes "Wrightsville," we learn that Johnny's What-are-you-rebelling-against?-Whad'-ya-got? amorphous nihilism is appealing to women, as sweet Kathie Bleeker discovers. It's a point that would not be lost when fascination with the outlaw biker lifestyle burgeoned.

American critics of *The Wild One* feared that the motorcycle-themed glamorization of nihilistic rebellion would prove influential, and they were absolutely right. The success of the film not only introduced the motorcycle rebel to the mainstream, but it also shaped the outlaw biker style and made it cool. And life imitated art. The Outlaw Motorcycle Club's "Charlie," the red-eyed skull over crossed pistons, is derived from Black Rebel costumes.[5] In fact, *The Wild One*, probably more than any other single event, was the catalyst for creating and codifying what would become one of the weirdest nihilist phenomena in American history—the outlaw biker.

---

[5] "Outlaws World," American Outlaws Association, www.outlawsmcworld .com, accessed 2004.

Nihilism and FTW Style

Outlaw bikers are not noted for their philosophical ruminations; their nihilism is, rather, a spontaneous symptom of modern culture. Recall how the nihilist perspective reveals that traditional values are worthless, and that ultimately nothing has any meaning. As Camus notes, one can deal with this meaninglessness by holding it in contempt. The outlaw biker lifestyle was conspicuously and outrageously contemptuous of the values the majority of American society embraced, seeing them as pathetic, phony, and suffocating.

As the outlaw motorcycle style evolved, club members were more likely to be marginalized working-class males than WWII veterans. This transition marks the beginnings of the hardcore, badass faction of American biker culture, the "one-percenters." The one-percenter motorcycle gangs gained notoriety in the 1960s, primarily as a result of the California Hells Angels' widely reported violent antics at Monterey and, later, Altamont. During this time, Hells Angel Sonny Barger became the chief spokesman of biker nihilism. A 1965 *Newsweek* interviewer noted that the unkempt Barger actually stank.[6] Nurturing a foul odor like this, Sigmund Freud said, can be understood as a direct assault on civilization.[7] And a cultivated stench was just one of many ploys of outlaw bikers for communicating their contempt for modern values.

Beyond stench and an inherently confrontational attitude, the outlaw biker style evolved an elaborate iconography to advertise nihilistic rebellion. Motorcycle gang insignia, for example, was designed to be shocking. Witness the Outlaws' "Charlie" and the Hells Angels' winged skulls. Black has archetypal associations with evil, and the black leather vest that sports the club insignia also carries artifacts associated with the individual member's attitude and experience. One might see Nazi death's heads, swastikas, DILLIGAF (Do I Look Like I Give a Fuck), DFFL (Dope Forever, Forever Loaded), FYYFF (Fuck You, You Fucking Fuck)—and the classic FTW (Fuck the World), a bit of slang uniquely associated with outlaw biker style.

---

[6] "The Wild Ones," *Newsweek* (29th March, 1965), p. 25.
[7] Sigmund Freud, *Civilization and Its Discontents* (New York: Norton, 1961), p. 46.

"Dangerous Motorcycle Gangs," a widely circulated two-hour police course, notes that a white cross on a biker's colors is earned by robbing a grave, a red cross by "committing homosexual fellatio with witnesses present."[8] Green wings denote the wearer performed cunnilingus on a venereally diseased woman, and purple wings signify—get this!—oral sex with a dead woman! (p. 32). As a rejection of values and an expression of nihilism, what could be more aberrant and grossly offensive? And even if these interpretations are inaccurate or fabricated by bikers themselves as a joke, they still reveal the outrage that the outlaw biker expression of nihilism intended to inspire. When we discover that everything is false, Nietzsche warned, we learn that *anything* is permitted.

All in all, the authors of "Dangerous Motorcycle Gangs" conclude, outlaw biker philosophy can be summarized by a single phrase: "fuck the world." "FTW," the report notes, "is their motto and is the arrogant attitude by which this subculture attains its goals and objectives. . . . They don't want to be like the normal citizen or dress like them. This is why they have created their own dress code which is filthy, repulsive, and often offensive" (p. 14).

And the rub of it, the authors seem to lament here, is that this despicable FTW style of nihilism makes the outlaw biker extraordinarily attractive to "good looking" women: "Strangely enough, an unlimited number of good-looking females, it seems, are attracted to the macho image . . . to a life which seems as exciting as a roller coaster ride, fast motorcycles, macho men, drugs, alcohol, parties, guns, topless bars, and anyway-you-want-it sex" (p. 23).

The Born Losers: Hollywood Tells It Like It Is . . . Sort Of

Of the various biker films spawned by the success of *The Wild One*—films with promising titles like *Devils' Angels*, *Cycle Savages*, *Death Riders*, *Hell Riders*, and *Moto Psycho*—none communicated the wanton destruction nihilism could evoke better than Tom Laughlin's *The Born Losers* (1967). In just thirteen

---

[8] "Dangerous Motorcycle Gangs," *An Inside Look at Outlaw Motorcycle Gangs* (Boulder: Paladin, 1992).

years, Hollywood took audiences from Johnny's rather tame, ruminative nihilism to nihilism as a titanic force of destruction. "Nihilism is . . . not only the belief that everything deserves to perish," said Nietzsche, "but one actually puts one's shoulder to the plough; *one destroys*" (p. 22). The Born to Lose Motorcycle Club does just that.

The club's membership consists of bleary-eyed psychopaths like "Cueball," "Gangrene," and "Crabs," who stumble from one kidnapping, gang rape, and bar brawl to another, all the while smashing what they can. There are no boundaries to their depravity or brutality, and there is utterly no rational motivation for their monstrous behavior.

Not surprisingly, the nihilistic rampage in *The Born Losers* comes to mind when reading the social analysis of Dimitri Pisarev, the nineteenth-century Russian who became a primary spokesman for a new political philosophy, *nihilism*: "Here is the ultimatum of our camp; what can be smashed should be smashed; what will stand the blow is good; what will fly into smithereens is rubbish; at any rate hit out right and left—there will and can be no harm from it."[9]

Motorcycle-Themed Nihilism:
A Billion-Dollar Fantasy

No matter how frightening or loathsome the outlaw biking style of nihilism appeared to be, it also had a mysterious resonance; and no matter how Hollywood might negatively dramatize the image of the outlaw biker as a chopper-riding psychotic in black leather and chains, it remained a heady, intoxicating fantasy. In *Hells Angels*, Hunter S. Thompson writes that outlaw bikers "command a fascination, however reluctant, that borders on psychic masturbation."[10] He's right. Middle America, always fascinated with bohemian ways, couldn't seem to get enough seamy reports of sex, depravity, filth, violence, and far-out choppers. Accordingly, the fantasy image of the badass nihilist biker slowly acquired almost mythic proportions as a symbol of rebel-

---

[9] Dimitri Pisarev, quoted in Avrahm Yarmolinsky's *Road to Revolution* (New York: Macmillan, 1959), p. 120.

[10] Hunter S. Thompson, *Hell's Angels* (New York: Ballantine, 1966), p. 262.

lion, metaphysical escape, and existential freedom. Finally, it was ripe for Madison Avenue.

Willie G. Davidson, grandson of one of Harley-Davidson's founders, played a major role in making nihilism trendy when he borrowed styling cues from the chopped and stripped-down bikes preferred by one-percenters. Until his bold move, Harley-Davidson made it clear that it loathed the image of nihilism the outlaw bikers cultivated. And whether or not Willie G.'s decision was motivated by the simple realization that if you can't fight 'em, join 'em, it was a stroke of marketing genius. The 1977 FXS Low Rider, introduced to the public in Daytona, tells the story: outlaw cool would be king at H-D. The Low Rider put Harley-Davidson back on the road and helped to mainstream FTW style.

With Harley-Davidson's turnaround, more and more motor-cycle manufacturers followed suit, marketing dozens of motor-cycles that attempted to model a tasteful flair of outlaw styling. In a relatively short twenty years, what was once reviled became normalized, and TV commercials and programs, video games, fashion, filmmakers, celebrities, athletes, and politicians have embraced the badass biker image. And in the last twenty years, coincidently, interest in motorcycling has grown dramatically with double-digit sales increases for nearly every manufacturer. The wild success of the Teutuls' *American Chopper* and other television programs like it is just one example of the mainstream appeal of the badass outlaw style.

Motorcycle advertising now routinely encourages consumers to abandon social conformity and celebrate the suppressed bar-barian, assuring them that this motorcycle or that accessory can communicate the FTW attitude, albeit tastefully. An ad for muf-flers, for instance, incorporates the image of a leather-clad, tat-too-covered biker emerging from under a three-piece suit and the line, "Inside every good guy there's a real badass." Ads encourage consumers to "Raise some hell," "Take the Low Road," pose the question "Who cares where you're going?" and remind them that "You've got the attitude" or "So much evil, so little time." "Ride like Hell, Feel Like Heaven" a motorcycle ad selling boots says.

Victory Motorcycle describes its new chopper-inspired "8 Ball" as "Beautiful as Sin. Raw, basic, and dark. Just what a black sheep should be." An advertisement for Ford's Harley-Davidson trucks (which tells you something about the power of the out-law image) offers surprising insight into the psychology of FTW cool: "It says, 'Look at Me' and 'What are you looking at?' simultaneously." Even the Hells Angels Motorcycle Club is now selling its 2005 calendar with outlaw biker pin-ups, big bruisers with menacing scowls, and, of course, tricked-out choppers. And Wal-Mart, known for refusing to market products it considers controversial, sells "chopper" bicycles and T-shirts with the iron cross motif, the latest symbol of outlaw chopperdom.

A Geico insurance ad is another clear indication about what happened when FTW attitude went commercial. It shows a huge biker, apparently a hard-core one-percenter complete with a shaved head, long gray goatee, black sleeveless tee, and an intimidating expression. Tattooed on his massive biceps is the cutsie Geico gecko. Of course, motorcycle insurance is antithetical to everything the FTW attitude represents—nihilists don't need no fuckin' insurance.

What's particularly revealing about the marketing of nihilistic sentiments is that all of the advertisements mentioned above appeared in *mainstream* motorcycling magazines, mags like *American Iron, Cycle World, Cruiser, Motorcyclist,* and *Ride.* One won't find nihilism shtick in magazines such as *Street Chopper, The Horse,* and *Outlaw* that ostensibly represent hard-core bikers.

"You Used to Hate Us, Now You Wanna Be Us": Bike Week Make-Believe

The enormous success of motorcycle-themed nihilism is nowhere more apparent than at biker extravaganzas held in Sturgis, Laconia, and Daytona. These massive, ten-day affairs are attended by hundreds of thousands of motorcycle riders who, at some level, can become "outlaws," in gigantic FTW-style fantasies featuring drinking, loud motorcycles, and the requisite symbols of outlawry, hedonism, and nihilism.

Consider that Daytona's Bike Week attracts 500,000 to 600,000 motorcycle fans, predominantly male and, in the last decade, primarily middle-aged and middle-class. And while locals rail against the perceived depravity of the affair, prohibitions regarding public drunkenness, decency, and safety are relaxed to support the FTW fantasy. Why? Nihilism chic pays.

According to Volusia County reports, Bike Week is worth about $340 million.

Evidence of the popularity of FTW style is everywhere at Bike Week. When the most famous outlaw, Sonny Barger, came to sign his autobiographical *Hell's Angel*, for example, hundreds waited in line for a copy. In addition to the Teutuls' Orange County Choppers, at least twenty chopper manufacturers set up shop during the week to promote their badass (and hardass . . .) rides. On Main Street, the heart of the affair, there is a new DILLIGAF store specializing in DILLIGAF accessories, where, with screaming irony, no smoking is allowed. Oh, and check out its online store, where you'll get a ten-percent discount. . . .

The few Bike Week participants who are actually one-percenters—the fashion aristocracy here—wear their colors. Most leather, however, merely mimics the outlaw biker style by sporting advertisements for one or another brand of motorcycle, patches and pins purchased at bars and boutiques featuring the outlaw style or handed out at toy runs and other charitable events organized for motorcyclists. It's no wonder that hardcore bikers lament the faddish popularity of their style:

> And what about what used to be the standard apparel? The plain black T-shirts, the engineer boots, jeans with the little battery acid holes. Remember them? Mostly all gone now. Each item replaced by its designer counterpart to impart a carefree sense of tasteful rebellion. In essence, nothing more than a costume that only gets put on to ride the bike. The vest was a place to hang your experiences. These days that $170 vest is nothing more than free ad space for Harley-Davidson.[11]

Images of the human skull are extraordinarily popular accessories, too. Skulls are the acknowledged touchstones of the entire biker world. As *memento mori* ("remember that you must die"), human skulls have historically symbolized our own mortality, and they're associated with poison, pirates, evil, and death. But since the advent of outlaw bikers, skulls are most often associated with the outlaw style, communicating danger, an attitude of reckless abandon, and FTW.

---

[11] "Arby," "See no Evo," *Full Throttle* (August #46, 1999), p. 86.

With the successful marketing of nihilism, however, the shock value of skulls has been rendered impotent by their ubiquity—they're *everywhere*, grinning, flaming, crying, smoking, scowling, screaming, rotting, jesting, exploding, and flying. Skull paint themes and graphics on custom bikes are everywhere, and even Harley-Davidson offers a factory custom paint job featuring flaming skulls. The number of skull-related products for accessorizing costumes and motorcycles is nothing short of amazing. Like so many other offensive trappings of outlaw nihilism, then, skulls have become conventional and stylish.

Since nihilism became fashionable, not surprisingly, hardcore bikers are alternately puzzled, amused, or annoyed by what's happened to biker gigs like Bike Week:

> Harleys have become a toy for every yuppie rub [rich urban biker] jerk off out there. They get to play "Biker" without havin' a clue what it's really all about. A half million people at Bike Week and maybe fifty thousand bikers at best. Like the t-shirt says, "You used to hate us, now you wanna be us." I just hope there's some of us around when they're gone.[12]

The great irony is that while tens of thousands at Bike Week shell out big money to ape the one-percenter style, it's a crowd that wants nothing to do with true nihilists. The fact is, that even within the context of Bike Week, most fantasy outlaw bikers would be afraid or embarrassed to be seen with true desperados. And when the party's over, FTW sentiments have to be returned to the closet, covered up, or garaged.

What's the Appeal of Biker Nihilism, Anyway?

Actual one-percenters should be admired, I suppose, for having the courage of their convictions. The price American society exacts from any iconoclast is extremely high, and higher still for the nihilist. The fact is, outlaw bikers are shunned by nearly everyone, banned from many businesses, and frequently harassed by police. And that's the irony: The rebellion and existential freedom associated with the outlaw lifestyle is actually demanding and heavily codified. Nihilism, too, contains its own

---

[12] "Frog," "The Readers Write," *Dixie Biker* (April 2001), p. 38.

curious irony: Holding the conviction that truth doesn't exist is difficult to justify because the statement "truth doesn't exist" *is* a truth. Paradoxically, pure nihilism is a position that destroys all positions—even itself.

So why has the FTW style struck a cord with otherwise mainstream motorcycle fans? From a psychological perspective, Freud would argue that, like a true nature's child, we were born to be wild. Unfortunately, for most of us, our superego won't let us walk on the wild side. So outlaw bikers, like criminals and mobsters, intrigue us, at least at a distance, because they can freely express their existential outrage and act on their aggressive and predatory impulses without guilt.[13]

From an existential perspective, rebellion can add zest to the life of the conventional herd animal saddled with responsibility, rules, political correctness, and groupthink sentiments. Rejecting this burden is liberating, the existentialists suggest, providing an escape from a pointless life led in quiet desperation. But even more gratifying, argue the nihilists, would be to smash everything. And if the growing popularity of the FTW style is any indication, even the fantasy of nihilism is a heady thing, suggesting that the burden of modern life is indeed becoming so painful, so distasteful as to be unbearable.

Nietzsche thought that civilization's struggle with nihilism was a necessary "pathological transitional phase" that would last two centuries (p. 14). We're about halfway now, so we can expect to see plenty more phenomena like the FTW biker lifestyle *and* the mainstream's fascination with it. Whether or not civilization will survive the battle with nihilism, the philosopher wasn't sure.

But let's face it, if one accepts the metaphysical realities nihilism reveals, we're all born to lose because life's a bitch and then we die. So let existentialism guide; *there's no fate that can't be surmounted by scorn.* And outlaw bikers have proven that the motorcycle can be a powerful talisman for releasing and expressing one's dissatisfaction with life. Free yourself from the meaningless demands of the herd, then. Be a badass outlaw biker. Fuck the world! On Saturday afternoons, anyway, after the yard is mown.

---

[13] Sigmund Freud, *On Narcissism*, reprinted in Joseph Sandler, *et al.*, eds., *Freud's "On Narcissism": An Introduction* (New Haven: Yale University Press, 1991), p. 19.

7

Harleys as Freedom Machines: Myth or Fantasy?

FRED FELDMAN

I've been on two wheels for over forty years. My earliest bikes were Indians—Chiefs and a Warrior. I also rode BSAs, Triumphs, and other assorted British bikes including a really beautiful Velocette Venom Veeline Clubman. But now as I enter the twilight of my riding years, I find myself sticking ever more tightly to my Harley—a nearly stock 1986 FXRT. I often wonder why I am so attached to my Harley; why I prefer to keep it rather than trading it for a smoother, faster, more modern machine from Japan or Germany. Why am I so attached to a Harley?

A possible answer is suggested by some Harley advertising. In the 1970s, the Motor Company inaugurated a new advertising campaign. The Harley-Davidson motorcycle was to be known as "The Great American Freedom Machine." The flag-waving carried on as usual, but with the added link to "freedom." The effects of the campaign linger. We are still given the opportunity to purchase belt buckles, wall clocks, tee shirts, beer mugs, cigarette lighters, and other assorted consumer goods proclaiming the intimate connection between Harleys and freedom. The advertising motto is suggestive, but the philosopher may be puzzled. What kind of freedom is being invoked here? And what is the alleged connection to Harleys? Could this explain my attachment to my FXRT? Do I ride a Harley because it makes me more free?

Freedom in the Abstract

Freedom, broadly construed, is fundamentally a matter of *absence of restriction, interference, or constraint.* You are completely free to do something if absolutely nothing prevents you from doing it. Limitations on your freedom come about when something interferes or restricts or puts extra costs on doing that thing. Those who tend to focus on political matters may think of freedom as *absence of legal or governmental restrictions* and they may naturally be inclined to think that when a person has a lot of freedom, there are relatively few legal restrictions on his speech, religion, travel, associations, and other sorts of activity that sometimes are restricted by governmental interference. But there are many other sorts of freedom. We can distinguish among these sorts of freedom by focusing on the source of the restriction. Who, or what, is making it harder, or impossible, for me to engage in this action?

Metaphysical Constraints on Action

A person's freedom might be limited by factors that are necessary and pervasive in nature. For example, suppose that the principle of universal causation is true, so that absolutely every event that occurs is caused by prior events. Nothing is genuinely "random." Then every bit of every person's behavior would be caused by prior events (and those events would be caused by events before them, and so on to the beginning of time). In a sense then, everyone would be completely "unfree." Your movements would be relevantly like the movements of a pushrod in a smoothly running Twin Cam 88B engine. And you would still be completely unfree in this way even if you steadily felt as if you could choose to behave in a different manner. The feeling of freedom, in this case, would be some sort of delusion—itself the product of earlier causes going back to times before you were born.

Some philosophers believe that pervasive metaphysical "unfreedom" would occur if there were a God who has had foreknowledge of every bit of human behavior from the moment of creation. They think divine foreknowledge would make it impossible for anyone ever to do anything other than what one in fact does. After all (they reason) if God already knew millions of years ago that I would neglect to wear my helmet today, then it is in a way impossible for me to put it on. How can I put it on, if He already knew millions of years ago that I wouldn't? Surely it is too late now for me to bring it about that He *didn't* know millions of years ago that I wouldn't wear my helmet.

Another alleged possible source of pervasive unfreedom would be "fate." Suppose it was already *true* millions of years ago that I would neglect to wear my helmet today. I can't change the past. So (some infer) it's impossible for me to wear my helmet today. If we are constrained in any of these necessary and pervasive ways, then each of us is *metaphysically unfree.* If there are no such metaphysical constraints on some person's performance of some action, then that person is *metaphysically free* to perform the action.

It should be obvious that if people do have this metaphysical freedom, then they have it whether they are cruising down the highway on a Road King or in a Toyota Camry LS. A person's choice of vehicle could not seriously be thought to have any bearing on the question whether she has metaphysical freedom. Indeed, it seems likely that if anyone is metaphysically free, then everyone is metaphysically free. Metaphysical freedom would be part of the human condition in general if it were part of anyone's condition. Surely, when the advertisers at the Motor Company decided to invoke the phrase "The Great American Freedom Machine," they did not mean to suggest that those who were formerly constrained by chains of causal determinism or divine foreknowledge could break those chains by buying a Fat Boy. If they were chained by metaphysical necessity before purchasing the bike, they would be so chained afterwards.

Legal Constraints on Action

A much less sweeping sort of restriction on action might be imposed by governments and legislation. For example, suppose that I live in a state where there are laws prohibiting the use of straight pipes. Then I am not legally free to use straight pipes. Legislative restrictions on freedom are not quite as overpowering as metaphysical restrictions. If you are metaphysically unfree to do something, then you simply cannot do it. But you can violate the law. You can install and use straight pipes even if there is a law against it. But then you will be subject to various legal penalties, such as a fine or jail time. The restrictions in this case appear in the form of extra costs or burdens associated with performing some sort of action.

Let's say that you are completely legally free to do something if there are absolutely no governmental, regulatory, or legal constraints on your doing it. To the extent that there are legal restrictions on your behavior, your level of legal freedom is reduced.

If a person lives in a place where there is a government in charge, then his legal freedom cannot be absolute. Consider my neighbors in New Hampshire. Their license plates proudly proclaim LIVE FREE OR DIE, yet even they cannot claim complete legal freedom. They must get their cars inspected and keep right except when passing. They are required by law to have the freedom-proclaiming plates clearly visible and illuminated on the backs of their cars. They are not completely legally free. A person's legal freedom is greater as the restrictions and requirements are less severe.

Over the vast range of interesting activities, choosing a Harley instead of a Camry has no impact at all on one's level of legal freedom. Harley riders and Camry drivers in the United States are equally legally free with respect to virtually every sort of behavior. Assuming that they are of equal age and citizenship, and that neither is a convicted felon, they are free to vote, to run for office, to engage in peaceful protest, to assemble with others of like mind, and to move about the country as they see fit. Neither of them is legally free to exceed the speed limit or to drive without a license. Neither of them is free to make threatening remarks about the President.

One would have to search carefully for any difference in levels of legal freedom between a Harley rider and a Camry driver. However, it seems that if we look closely enough, we may find that there are some microscopic differences. In most states Harley riders enjoy slightly less legal freedom than drivers of Toyota Camrys. The mere fact that a person chooses to ride a motorcycle subjects him to extra governmental interference. In Massachusetts (where I live) anyone who wants to operate a motor vehicle on a public road must first have a regular driver's license. We all uniformly face that limitation on our freedom. But those who want to ride a motorcycle face even further restrictions. We must take extra tests, both on the road and in the classroom. And, worst of all, we are required to wear approved helmets.

I recognize, of course, that we are legally free to ride our bikes without seatbelts. That is a restriction that limits the freedom of car drivers, but one that we evade. Nevertheless, in spite of some minor differences, on balance it seems to me that there is no basis for saying that the Harley rider is any more legally free than the Camry driver.

Circumstantial Constraints on Action

Some restrictions on action have nothing to do with laws, and nothing to do with universal causation or any other pervasive metaphysical factor. Such restrictions might arise from some mere matter of personal circumstances. For example, suppose you live on an isolated farm. You have no car, truck, or motorcycle. There is no bus station nearby. You can't afford to call a cab. If you want to go anywhere, you will have to walk, but the nearest interesting city is many miles away. Then your freedom to travel is restricted, even if you have free will and there is no law against traveling. The problem is the mere circumstance of not having access to a suitable vehicle. Let's use the term "circumstantial freedom" to refer to the sort of freedom that is restricted in this way by circumstances.

In this situation, a Harley might be a "freedom machine." If you could get your hands on a bike, you could toss some gear into the saddlebags and cruise away into the sunset, looking for adventure. The Harley would open up some options that would otherwise have remained closed.

Thus, it might seem that the Harley has earned the right to be called "The Great American Freedom Machine."

But there is a serious problem with this line of thought. We seem to be comparing the case in which you have no means of transportation with the case in which you have a Harley. Of course your freedom to travel is greater in the second case. But the fact that the vehicle in this case is a Harley is irrelevant. Your freedom to travel would be similarly increased if you managed to get your hands on an Indian, or a flathead Ford, or a Toyota Camry. *Any* suitable vehicle would improve your situation freedom-of-travel-wise. So the example does not show that *Harleys* are freedom machines; it suggests that *cars, trucks, motorcycles, or any other suitable vehicles* are freedom machines.

In his dialogue *Philebus*, Plato (427–347 B.C.E.) compared the life of pleasure with the life of wisdom, trying to see which would be the better life. In the dialogue, Socrates lays down some ground rules for comparison: he says that to get a fair comparison you need to compare a life containing lots of pleasure but totally devoid of wisdom to a life containing lots of wisdom but totally devoid of pleasure. We should follow Socrates. We should compare a life containing just a Harley (and no other vehicle) to a life containing just a Toyota Camry LS (and no other vehicle). We should try to imagine the lives vividly and fairly, and we should try to determine whether either life is significantly freer than the other. Does possession of the Harley open up options that would be closed to the Camry driver? Or is it the other way round? Or are the two drivers pretty much on a par when it comes to freedom?

It's hard to see how Harley ownership could have a significant effect on circumstantial freedom. Some small differences are obvious: if you don't have a Harley, you are not free to walk into your garage, throw your leg over your Harley, and fire it up. So the Harley owner has freedom to do one thing that the Camry owner cannot do. But the Camry owner has an equal advantage with respect to another sort of action: he is free to walk into his garage, slide his butt into the front seat of his Camry, and fire it up. The Harley owner can't do that. It seems to be a zero sum game. Whichever way you go, you win one, and you lose one.

Some people use the term "freedom machine" to refer to wheelchairs. This seems to me to make a lot of sense—especially if we think of the sort of freedom that involves the removal of circumstantial restrictions on actions. Without a wheelchair, a person with a physical disability may be restricted, or limited, in his movements. There are places he can't go, or can go only with difficulty. But when he gets a suitable wheelchair, previously closed options open up. The number of interesting alternatives available to him increases. Nothing like this happens when a Camry driver trades in his car for a Sportster.

Harleys and the Expression of Freedom

There's no clear conception of freedom according to which riding a Harley will lead to an increase in someone's actual level of freedom. But it's still possible that there is some connection between Harleys and freedom. Maybe the idea is not that owning a Harley will *make you* more free. Maybe the idea is that owning a Harley will give you an opportunity to *celebrate*, or *express*, your freedom. As you cruise around the neighborhood with your straight pipes rumbling, you might in a way *proclaim* your freedom. Every ride could be construed as a sort of exclamation: "Look at me! I'm free! My activities are subject to fewer constraints than the activities of Camry drivers! Whoopie!"

Surely a person could do that. But in light of what we have already seen, this seems a bizarre way of expressing your freedom. After all, if you choose to ride a Harley, you will not be any more free in any identifiable way, and you will be slightly less free in some ways. Isn't it somewhat paradoxical to express your freedom by doing something that is antithetical to your freedom? It seems as bizarre as celebrating your health by eating greasy french fries and sugarcoated donuts, or celebrating your happy marriage by running around with strange women (or strange men, as the case may be).

Harleys and the Feeling of Freedom

Many riders claim to get and enjoy the "feeling of freedom" while riding. Perhaps this is closer to the point of Harley's motto. Maybe what they really mean is "Harley-Davidson: the Great American Feeling-of-Freedom Machine."

But this idea is also problematic. The central problem, as I see it, is that it's not clear that there is any such feeling. Let's consider this.

Try to imagine the feeling of fatigue. If you are fatigued, and you reflect on how you feel, may notice certain typical and familiar (if hard to describe) sensations: minor aches and pains in some joints; weakness in some muscles; droopiness in the eyelids; an urge to take a nap. Similar things happen when you feel hot or cold, or bored or excited, or dizzy. There are certain sensations that you typically have when you are in these states. If X is some state or condition (fatigue, coldness, fear, etc.), then the feeling of X is the combination of sensations you typically have when you are in state or condition X.

But there is no typical set of sensations that goes along with being free. Suppose, for example, that you have been locked in a jail cell for a long time. Suppose that during the night, while you slept, someone unlocked the door. When you wake up in the morning, you would be free but you would feel nothing distinctive. Freedom itself has no "feel."

Suppose you check the door and discover that it's unlocked. Now you believe that you are free. (Note that the *belief* that you are free is not a feeling; it's a belief.) Perhaps when you think you are free you have a special feeling of freedom, and maybe this special feeling of freedom is the one that allegedly makes Harley riding so wonderful.

Although I have studied my feelings while riding, I never felt anything that I would describe as "the feeling of freedom." Vibration, yes. (I used to ride a Sportster.) Cold, yes. Heat, yes. Buffeting of wind, yes. But freedom, no. Talk about the "feeling of freedom" seems to me to be based on a failure to reflect with sufficient care upon one's own psychological states. Perhaps the Harley advertisements have led us down the garden path to the point where we misdescribe our own experience.

Often when I'm riding, I feel happy. I may have a feeling of exhilaration. I'm glad to be out on my bike. But feelings of happiness or exhilaration should not be confused with the feeling of freedom. I wonder if riders who claim to experience "the feeling of freedom" in fact have an experience that contains not a *feeling*, but rather a *belief* about freedom. Maybe what they experience is the combination of a feeling of happiness with a belief—the belief that they are free; the belief that they can "do anything" while riding. How paradoxical! They are in fact a little bit less free than they would have been if they had chosen a Camry; there is slightly less that they can do. They can't easily change the track on their current CD; they can't comfortably sip a cup of coffee at 75 m.p.h.; they can't fiddle with the controls on their AC. They could do these things if they were driving a Camry. Yet they feel happy because they think they are more free.

If my hunch is right, this talk of Harleys as Feeling-of-Freedom Machines is thus doubly mistaken. First, the relevant feeling is not the feeling of freedom. It's the feeling of happiness. Second, the associated belief—the belief that you are more free on your Harley—is probably false.

If Not Freedom, then What?

The old notion that we ride Harleys because Harleys are freedom machines simply won't cut it. If taken as the view that riding a Harley will make you more free, it's false. If taken as the view that riding a Harley will give you the feeling of freedom, then it's unclear and dubious. Is there any such "feeling"? So there must be some other reason why we ride. We evidently give up some of our freedom in exchange for other goods. What are these goods?

Some say it's the comradery. They join their local HOG chapter hoping to gain solidarity with a bunch of biker brothers. This seems like a pretty expensive and inconvenient way to get friends, especially if you really don't enjoy riding all that much. Surely, if you are looking for friends, it would be more efficient and convenient just to post some personals. Personally, I don't ride because of loneliness.

Perhaps in an earlier era, owning a Harley gave our grandfathers the opportunity to travel to distant places cheaply and efficiently. But the idea that travel by Harley is cheap and efficient in America in the twenty-first century is ludicrous. If you want to get someplace cheaply and efficiently, the Camry is the ticket—especially in cold and rainy weather. There are any number of Japanese motorcycles that will run circles around your Harley. So if you want to get there *fast*, you should get something more like a Suzuki GSXR 1300R.

Some say that the great thing about a Harley is that it gives you the chance to smell the roses. This much is true: when you pass through a neighborhood where there are a lot of roses, you may be able to smell them while riding a Harley. However, if the smell of roses turns you on, you can also get your turn-on in a Camry. Just press the button that opens the windows. (The Harley has a drawback not shared by the Camry: when you rumble through a neighborhood where there is a sewage treatment plant, you will be forced to smell the shit. You can't close the windows on the Harley. Nor can you turn up the air conditioner. In this case the Camry has the edge.)

Some people get a lot of satisfaction from knowing that they can personally dismantle and reconstruct their vehicle with their own tools. They enjoy knowing that they understand what makes it work. In some cases they take great pride in knowing that they designed and built the machine on which they ride. If you want that, you might get it with an antique bike, or with a Ford 8n tractor, but not with a Harley of recent vintage, which is as incomprehensible as a Toyota.

My own view (and here I acknowledge that I am speaking only for myself) is that traveling on a Harley is just more fun and more exciting than going in a cage. I like the thrilling feeling when I dip into a nicely banked curve, and feel the power and ease of the bike as it leans until the footpeg begins ever so slightly to skim the pavement. I enjoy many sensory aspects of the experience: the sound of the exhaust, the feeling of the air and the engine, the look and smell of the bike. I also enjoy the excitement that comes when I sweep around a corner and discover a flock of turkeys in the road, or a moose standing there dumbfounded. That sort of thing may give you something to think about; something to remind you of the fact that you love life, and love being close to your machine, and love the thrill that comes from riding a bit closer to the edge.

Of course, I could get those pleasures on a Honda or a BMW. But I also take pleasure in knowing that my bike is the direct descendant of a long line of air-cooled V-twins going back through the Panheads, Shovelheads, Knuckleheads, and Flat Heads all the way back to the Model J and the 5D and then even further back to the (single cylinder) Silent Grey Fellow. My bike links me to a great tradition that started in a garage in Milwaukee more than a century ago, and I enjoy knowing that I am part of that tradition. These are all delightful experiences; they are some of my reasons for riding a Harley. They are pleasures you can't get in a car or on any bike but a Harley. But they have nothing to do with freedom.

If you continue to believe that there is some connection between Harleys and freedom, then I encourage you to think more deeply. To say that riding a Harley makes you more free is to say that riding a Harley removes some restrictions or constraints on your choices of action. Can you identify the source of the restrictions precisely? Can you specify the forms of action that become available when you plunk down your $20,000 for the Harley? Perhaps you think riding your Harley gives you a feeling of freedom. Can you say precisely what this feeling feels like? Can you identify the part of your body in which you feel it? Are you certain it's not just a belief combined with a feeling

of exhilaration? If not, maybe you should agree with me that while you wouldn't trade your Harley for a Camry, your preference has nothing to do with freedom.[1]

---

[1] Thanks to Elizabeth Feldman, Dick Godsey and Chris Heathwood for helpful criticism and suggestions.

8

From Spare Part to High Art: The Aesthetics of Motorcycles

CRAIG BOURNE

Sexy, beautiful, breathtaking, elegant, striking, magnificent, charismatic, iconic. Anyone who knows anything about bikes knows that some if not all of these terms truly apply to certain motorcycles. Even Europeans like myself, who aren't traditionally attracted to the cruiser style, could not help but be drawn to the Harley-Davidson V-Rod. And this is regardless of the fact that it has more power than the average Harley—it's simply because it's a stunning looking machine. Similarly, the Ducati 916, the work of designer Massimo Tamburini, was unveiled in the early '90s, stirring emotions that cannot simply be explained by noting its subsequent domination (with the help of its equally desirable successors, the 996 and the 998) of the World Superbikes competition. After all, other brands such as Honda did well in this competition, and yet didn't adorn as many bedroom walls (of middle-aged boys as much as the teenaged variety) as the Ducati superbike. In any case, even before it got on the track, the 916 was (and still is) seen as something special: those ignorant of its role—never mind its importance!—on the track are rarely insensitive to the delicious sight of the twin mufflers of the upswept exhaust system tucked under the rider's seat, the irresistible, somewhat sinister, set of headlights set into the droop-snoot nose of the front fairing, the mouth-watering styling of the tank, and the ultra clean look of the tubular trellis chassis and single-sided swinging arm. I could go on.

Of course, the Harley V-Rod and the Ducati superbikes are not the only examples: the heart-stopping back end of the MV Agusta F4, let alone the rest of the bike (also designed by the

genius Tamburini), is enough for even the coldest of fish to con-
template selling their children in order to put down a deposit on
one. And so it goes for many great bikes. It is beyond doubt,
then, that certain bikes are highly desirable objects, albeit to a
relatively small—that is, discerning!—group of people. The
question I wish to discuss is whether, to what extent, and, most
interestingly, *how* certain bikes function as genuine *works of art*,
where I use the phrase "work of art" to positively endorse an
object as worthy of aesthetic appreciation. (I confess that I have
a particular fetish for Italian brands and think that my case clearly
applies to many of these bikes. But those with an interest—
healthy or otherwise—in a different style, be it an American
cruiser, a Japanese high performer, or a classic British invention,
will be able to use my considerations to make the case for their
own objects of affection.)

I suspect that for anyone reading this piece, I'm already
preaching to the converted; but the controversy that surrounded
the motorcycle exhibition *The Art of the Motorcycle* at the Solomon
R. Guggenheim Museum, New York (June 26th–September 20th,
1998), the Field Museum of Natural History, Chicago (November
7th, 1998–March 21st, 1999), Guggenheim Museum Bilbao
(November 24th, 1999–September 3rd, 2000), and Guggenheim
Las Vegas (Autumn, 2001), is enough to show that it is not readily accepted that motorcycles are legitimate candidates for the title
work of art.[1] Some may think that the very fact that the bikes have
been exhibited in a museum confer on them the status of works
of art.[2] But there are plenty of objects exhibited in museums for
their historical value; so a case would have to be made for thinking that their aesthetic value, if they have any, is the reason for
the exhibition. And, in any case, this seems to get the explanation
the wrong way round: objects are exhibited because they are considered works of art, and not considered works of art because
they are exhibited. After all, we wouldn't say that had Picasso not
exhibited *Guernica* (1937), it would not have been a work of art.
Nor do we think that just because Paul McCartney or Prince
Charles exhibits his paintings that they are works of art.

---

[1] T. Krens, *et al.*, *The Art of the Motorcycle* (New York: Guggenheim Museum
Publications, 2001).
[2] See George Dickie, "Defining Art," *American Philosophical Quarterly* 6 (1969),
pp. 253–56.

However, the issue is not as straightforward as this. In a 2004 poll of five hundred British art experts (artists, critics, curators and the like), Marcel Duchamp's *Fountain* (1917), which consists of a urinal with "R. Mutt" (the name of a firm of sanitary engineers) signed on it, was considered, with 64 percent of the vote, the most influential work of the twentieth century, ahead of Picasso's *Les Demoiselles d'Avignon* (1907) with 42 percent, and Warhol's *Marilyn* (1964) with 29 percent. *Fountain* would not ordinarily have been considered as art (nor even anti-art) had it not been put forward as an object for our contemplation in such a setting. Duchamp followed the idea that any old object can be the object of aesthetic contemplation to its logical conclusion: what are we to say of the "readymade" urinal? If we find aesthetic value in an object whose sole function is for men to piss in, the very notion of a work of art, we would think, must be as empty as Duchamp's bladder. And yet *Fountain* became an icon of modern art. *That* is the profound paradox which lies at the heart of much modern art; and so arguably does deserve to be voted the most influential "work" of the twentieth century.

There is, then, a subtle complexity concerning the relationship between given works and their featuring in established institutions of the art world. But it is one that we need not get into. For it seems to me that the motorcycles featured in art galleries are not presented as any kind of anti-art or as an attempt at postmodern irony. Of course, some may take it to be a statement that any old object can be considered as an object of aesthetic contemplation. But if so, Duchamp did it first, and did it better. It is doubtful, then, that this can be the point (although, admittedly, Warhol's *Brillo Boxes* [1964] and Emin's *My Bed* [1999] are later variations on this theme; so why not the motorcycles?). Maybe the point is to advertise and make less alien the idea of a museum to the great unwashed who are the motorcycling community *via* some lowbrow objects intellectually accessible to them? (I say more about the assumptions behind this suggestion below.) Or maybe it's just to make some money? But whether or not there is some truth in these suggested motivations, none of them are primary reasons for the exhibitions. For there may be something rather eccentric about the Harley-Davidson Easy Rider Chopper with its Stars and Stripes painted tank, and its being exhibited in an art museum may be seen to be as postmodern a statement as Jasper Johns's American flags paintings of the 1950s.

tude that we must take towards a bike such that it counts as seeing it as an aesthetic object as opposed to something else? There is a tradition, of which the philosopher Immanuel Kant (1724–1804) is part, which takes "disinterest" as the characteristic attitude involved in aesthetic contemplation, where "disinterest" means that we have no interest in the *practical* uses of the object.[3]

Is disinterestedness, in this sense, the sort of attitude we take towards evaluating bikes? If it isn't, then we can't be evaluating the bike aesthetically, according to this theory. Luckily, though, we *can* adopt such an attitude towards bikes: *I* did it when searching around for my first bike! I didn't need one for traveling around. I wasn't even really aware of the sensual pleasures generated by twisting the throttle, leaning into corners, or braking heavily at high speed to reach crawling pace in a matter of a few seconds. No, I just fell in love with the *look* of the Ducati Monster; I bought one *primarily on the basis of its styling*. So not only is the disinterested attitude possible when contemplating bikes; it actually happens. And not just to me: in my experience, merely parking a Ducati in the street can draw a crowd of admirers who will just stand and stare for longer than they know they really should. The Harley V-Rod parked down the road has as many admirers.

The notion of disinterest also seems to capture to a certain extent our aesthetic *experience*: for when we are fully absorbed in an object such as a beautiful bike, we do feel a certain detachment from the world of practical affairs.

But it isn't just the appearance of the bike that grounds the aesthetic evaluation of it. In order to aesthetically appreciate the object fully, certain contexts of evaluation have to be invoked, such as its history, the means by which it was produced, and other objects of its kind. Now, although not many people are aware of these contexts in any detail, they are at least aware of other things on offer to look at, and that there is something extraordinary, relative to the others, about the particular object before them. As David Daiches argues in the case of literature, in order to develop an aesthetic appreciation of objects, we need to encounter and engage with a wide range

---

[3] Immanuel Kant, *Critique of Judgement* (Oxford: Clarendon, 1952 [1790]).

of possibilities: aesthetic appreciation is essentially comparative.[4] And we can add that, because there is more or less to
know about the contexts of evaluation as much as the internal
structure of the work itself, aesthetic appreciation also comes by
degrees. After all, to me the Ducati Monster still looks so much
better than other bikes in the "urban warrior" style (a comparative context of evaluation). But it emerges as an even more
remarkable achievement when we learn that it is over ten years
old and still going strong, and that it initiated the explosion of
bikes produced in this style from other manufacturers (an historical context of evaluation).

But even if we add these contexts of evaluation, I think the
attitude of disinterest is an inappropriate attitude to take towards
bikes if we require a complete aesthetic appreciation of them. I
shall argue for this in the last section.

For the time being, however, suppose we accept that this
sketch of the aesthetic attitude is fundamentally correct. We still
come across the problem of *taste*. In general, there does not
seem to be a special sense by which we perceive aesthetic properties, such as the beauty, elegance, or garishness of objects.
What we see are various arrangements of the component parts,
from which we make aesthetic judgments. Now, it is common
for people to disagree in their judgments concerning the aesthetic properties of an object, which makes some believe that it
is an entirely subjective matter: if someone claims that the
Honda Gold Wing is an elegant bike, whereas someone else
claims that it is one of the ugliest contraptions on the road, then
there is no fact of the matter as to who is correct. You'll hear
people say, "It's just a matter of taste."

But more needs to be said to make this position palatable, as
the philosopher David Hume (1711–1776) pointed out.[5] For I
think many of us would be reluctant to call the Gold Wing "elegant." We'd be wondering: according to *which* criteria could
someone judge it to be elegant? Yes, it is comfortable for long
journeys, smooth, useful, it allows for good communication

---

[4] D. Daiches, "Literary Evaluation," in J.P. Strelka, ed., *Problems of Literary Evaluation*, Yearbook of Comparative Criticism, Volume 2 (University Park: Pennsylvania State University Press, 1969).
[5] David Hume, "Of the Standard of Taste" [1757], in S. Feagin and P. Maynard, eds., *Aesthetics* (Oxford: Oxford University Press, 1997), pp. 350–364.

between rider and pillion, it has a reverse gear, and so on. And we'd check that this wasn't just what they meant by "elegant." But if they claimed that it really wasn't that and they genuinely thought it was elegant in the disinterested sense sketched above, we'd have to show them other bikes and compare their responses to them in order to get a feel for what they meant, and to check they really did have a good knowledge of how elegant bikes can be. But if after establishing that they meant by "elegant" what we meant, and that they had as much knowledge of bikes as we had, then we'd have nothing more to say, and all that there would be left to do would be to get on our respective bikes and continue on our way.

This seems to me to be correct. We are rightly irritated by those who make aesthetic judgments (often very loudly) concerning things of which they evidently know nothing at all. Hume's view accords with this feeling that the philistines are wrong, for it allows us to have genuine disagreement about something, and for there to be objective criteria by which we evaluate the merits of the respective positions: it isn't the case that "anything goes" in aesthetic evaluations: some people are better informed than others. But among those who are equally informed, a respectful acknowledgement of differences seems to be the right approach.

We've arrived at the conclusion, then, that motorcycles can be objects of aesthetic contemplation. But this is only half the task, since that conclusion alone doesn't show us what sort of art objects they are: *how* do they work as art objects; what is their nature as works of art?

By far the best way to proceed is to accept that some objects are paradigm cases of works of art: if anything is a work of art, then these things are. We can then use them to discuss what the relevant similarities and differences are between these paradigm cases and bikes, in order to determine their nature as works of art.

The Problem of Many Motorcycles: A Proliferation of Artworks or the Dissemination of One?

What are the paradigm art forms that share structural similarities with bikes? We have so far been talking about the aesthetics of bikes in terms of their visual appearance. Perhaps, then, we should liken them to paintings? But if we do, we come across the following problem: according to the philosopher Richard Wollheim, painting by its very nature produces a *unique* object (for example, a certain arrangement of acrylics on a particular canvas) that we identify as the art object. However, although there are one-off bikes, the majority of those we are considering as art works are mass produced: there are *many* instances of the Ducati 916. Think of people going to the Louvre in order to see *Mona Lisa*: it is essential to seeing the work of art that we see *that* instance, whereas when people went to visit the exhibitions at the Guggenheim museums, any old Ducati 916 would have done in order for them to appreciate the Ducati 916—it's not as if the first Ducati 916 has any more standing in this regard than the last one produced. Put it this way, if we were to burn *Mona Lisa*, the artwork itself would be destroyed, whereas if we crashed a Ducati 916, we could buy another or borrow a good friend's (so long as we didn't keep doing it . . .).

We might respond, however, that *Mona Lisa*, even though it doesn't, *could* have had many instances. If this were true, it wouldn't matter that there are many instances of certain bikes: this fact alone would not rule out a comparison between bikes and paintings. The philosopher Gregory Currie in *An Ontology of Art* disagrees with Wollheim that painting produces essentially a unique physical object.[6] According to Currie, a work of art is a *type of action* which produces such objects as paint on canvas. Since the work of art is a *type* of action, it could have been done by anyone at any time, just as much as *changing some sparkplugs* is a type of action which can be done on many different occasions by different people. So, even though Leonardo da Vinci was the only one to produce the physical object which we call "*Mona Lisa*" in the way that he did, someone else could have acted to produce a qualitatively identical object in the same way, and thus produced another instance of that work of art. It might be highly unlikely for this to happen; but that's not to say that it couldn't happen.

But even if we accept that the number of instances of the work does not matter to its being likened to painting, there is a

---

[6] G. Currie, *An Ontology of Art* (London: Macmillan, 1989).

fundamental difference between bikes and paintings: there is an intimate relationship between the artist and the instance of the work produced: *the artists themselves* have to apply the paint in order for it to be *their* work. This is certainly not the case in the production of a bike: Massimo Tamburini did not have to build each Ducati 916 in order for us to recognize it as being his work. So painting, even though it is a visual art form, is not the paradigm we're after.

But we need not look far for art forms which are similar to bikes in these respects: both literature and music (and film, if we want a visual element) allows for many instances of each of the works to exist, and neither art form requires that the artist execute each of the instances. Books that we buy are instances of the art works of the authors, and we can liken the printers of these books to the spray painters and mechanical and electrical engineers who put bikes together. In this respect, then, there is only one work of art which is the Ducati 916, just as there is only one novel which is *Nausea*. Both have many instances manufactured by many people, yet we see the works as the remarkable achievements of Tamburini and Jean-Paul Sartre, respectively.

This is a nice account, since it accords with our wanting to evaluate the art work as an achievement of the artist, given the contexts of evaluation mentioned above. The thing that might make philosophers queasy, however, is the status of the art work on this account. What *is* it? According to this view, it *isn't* each instance of it. After all, we don't think it is much of an artistic achievement to produce the thousandth Harley V-Rod. Neither do we think that Sartre's original manuscript for *Nausea* has any more claim to be the work of art than the copy on my shelf. (If it did, Sartre's spelling mistakes and handwriting, as well as the fact that he wrote in French, would have to be present in all instances of the work. This is clearly wrong.) Of course, Sartre's manuscript does have more historical, sentimental, and economic value, and Sartre might even have had such remarkable handwriting that it was itself aesthetically valuable; but these considerations are irrelevant to the evaluation of the *content* of the manuscript, that is, the novel itself. The same goes for the first (as well as the last ever) instance of the Harley V-Rod.

So what *is* the work of art? Seen as a type of action by an artist, it seems to have become a rather mysterious thing, unlike the tangible instances of it on which we can burn some rubber, pull wheelies, and pose. But since we are quite happy with the notion of a type of action in general, like *changing the spark-plugs*, we can leave this issue to the philosophers to resolve, and needn't, for our purposes, lose too much sleep over it.

From Spare Part to *High* Art?

Even if some people would be willing to make the concession that bikes can be art works, there will be a lot of them that would be unwilling to place them up there with other more conventional art forms. They might say, "Sure, call it art if you like, but it ain't no *high* art." Do such seemingly cultured people have a real distinction in mind, or is it more that they have a personal agenda (to keep some people in their place and indicate social or intellectual status, or some such)? Part of the controversy over having bikes exhibited in art galleries was no doubt due to the distinction between "high" and "low" art—bikes, being of the low variety, have no place in galleries. Paradigm cases of "high" art are classical music, ballet, and poetry, whereas rock music, breakdancing, and stand-up comedy are associated with "low" art. But, it seems to me, the distinction has no real basis; or at least, has no useful function. (I'll leave aside the separate sociological question as to why some people feel the need to draw the distinction.)

Is the distinction between good and bad art, with high art being good, and low art being bad? It can't be: although there is some sublime classical music, there also exists tediously bland and highly derivative works (Mozart being an example of someone who has produced music from both categories). And on the other side, there is some extraordinarily complex, exciting, and original rock music (consider the genre known as "progressive rock," which has fruitfully developed beyond its rather self-indulgent beginnings, or even the slightly more mainstream but thoroughly astonishing guitar work by Brian May on the Queen albums of the 1970s).

In *Popular Culture and High Culture*, sociologist Herbert Gans relates the notions of high and low art to that of high and low cultures, which itself is related to socioeconomic position.[7]

---

[7] H. Gans, *Popular Culture and High Culture* (New York: Basic Books, 1974).

But if this were right, it would be a surprise that a Cambridge University lecturer like myself could be an avid consumer of rock and jazz music, stand-up comedy, and television, as well as classical music and painting, but not care much for poetry and theatre. But, of course, it isn't.

Some characterize the distinction by saying that low art is (a) mass produced (at least the instances, or copies of the instances, are), (b) formulaic, (c) accessible, (d) requires only passive reception, and (e) is too involved with economic and social pressures to have the required autonomy that works of art have. But these criteria cut across the high-low distinction as usually characterized in terms of different art forms and genres: (a) I'd bet that more people have heard Beethoven's Fifth Symphony than have seen a Harley V-Rod; (b) much rock and jazz music is not formulaic, but in any sense in which some of it is (in, say, its use of a twelve-bar blues), some classical music is just as subject to the charge (such as, for instance, the widespread use of the cycle of fifths in Baroque music); (c) the use of classical pieces in television advertisements and the popularity of poster prints of modern paintings indicates that accessibility to a large extent is likely to be a function of how familiar a particular work is, rather than as something intrinsic to painting or classical music; (d) given the ubiquity of such works in popular culture, they are as passively received as any "low" art, although, it must be said, to appreciate any art work fully requires active participation at some level and an awareness of its setting within a context; and (e) Mozart was one of many who famously composed much work to please his benefactors, whereas there is a substantial network of independent record labels who specialize in promoting pioneering rock and jazz musicians without compromising the integrity of their work.

In a nutshell, it is rather ridiculous to make such a distinction between high and low art, if it's supposed to capture some intrinsic difference in quality across art forms (how can painting be better than comedy?), or within the same art form but across genres (how can Gregorian chant be better than jazz-rock fusion?). But denying that there is any real basis for the distinction is not to say that anything goes: we can still say, as we should want to, that within a given genre, some art works are better than others. What we can't say is that if bikes are works of art, then they are immediately of a lower status than other art forms. So, whether it is a good art piece or not has to be based on its *particular* merits against a context of evaluation, as we've already discussed.

Yet there may still be some nagging doubt that bikes are not genuine works of art. That's because we do not yet know how we are supposed to evaluate them as art objects, and that's because I have not yet identified the art form to which they are most allied. So that's what I'll now do.

What's It All About?

There are some, for instance, the philosopher Arthur Danto, who think that what is characteristic of a work of art is that some message must be put across such that it requires some kind of interpretation on the part of someone observing the work.[8] In other words, the work has to be *about* something; and perhaps the most satisfying art pieces are those that require some difficult probing in order to determine what that thing is. If this is true, then it is odd to consider bikes to be works of art, since it is not obvious that they are about *anything*, let alone anything deep.

But this isn't a particularly strong reason for not taking bikes to be works of art. First of all, it is not clear that works of art, as we ordinarily understand the notion, need to be *about* anything at all. Certainly, the majority of literary works are about something and require some interpretation. But Hugo Ball, a contributor to the early-twentieth-century *avant-garde* art movement known as *Dada*, produced entirely abstract "phonetic poetry," some of which begins:

gadji beri bimba
glandridi lauli lonni cadori

This clearly lacks meaning in the usual sense of the word. At most, we can say that it is about *itself* (in the sense that it is just about the sound and rhythm of the words used), but it is certainly not a candidate for any interpretation beyond this. Of

---

[8] A. Danto, *Transfiguration of the Commonplace* (Cambridge, Massachusetts: Harvard University Press, 1981); *After the End of Art* (Princeton: Princeton University Press, 1997).

course, you would quite naturally feel the need to discover the meaning behind the action of anyone who performed the poem, given its bizarreness, and there might be some profound point trying to be conveyed in using those words in that way; but this is distinct from what the poem itself is about.

Dada pieces, however, are considered by many to be more "anti-art" than art, and so may not fit our idea of a paradigm case of an art work.[9] But we need not look far for relatively unproblematic works of art which are not about anything. Paintings, for instance, often need to be interpreted in order for us to determine what they mean, but Piet Mondrian's famous series of "neo-plastic" paintings, where he limits himself to rectangular forms, primary colors and black, white, and grey, or the paintings of Mark Rothko, where there are large rectangular expanses of color arranged vertically with hazy edges, resulting in a vibrant, pulsating image, show that paradigm cases of art works need not be about anything (other than the art work itself, and perhaps also reference other art works). (The fact that an art work might invoke a particular emotion in the observer does not show that it is *about* that feeling, any more than someone telling you the price of an MV Agusta is *about* the emotions you feel when your dreams are crushed.) In any case, anyone who knows anything about music knows that it is implausible to think that all music represents or is about something (other than itself and perhaps other pieces of music), and so will wonder what all this fuss is about concerning abstract art anyway.

But rather than say that motorcycles are not about anything, and need not be about anything in order to be works of art, I'd rather say that motorcycles *are* about something, namely, *motorcycles.* Just as some music is just about the arrangement of sounds, and some painting is about the arrangement of shapes and colors, motorcycles are about the arrangement of motorcycle parts.

There are, however, two seeming disanalogies here. First, *some* music and *some* paintings *are* about something external to them, whereas *no* motorcycles are. Second, motorcycles cannot be arranged any old way, but there are no such prior constraints

---

[9] H. Richter, *Dada: Art and Anti-Art* (London: Thames and Hudson, 1964).

on music and painting. (There are certain constraints to which one must conform if the work is to be recognized as falling within a particular style or form. But artists have a choice over which constraints, if any, they impose on themselves, which is not the case when conceiving of a motorcycle.)

The first objection is easily dealt with, since it is not essential to a motorcycle that it not make reference to something outside of itself (and other motorcycles). After all, as will be well known to American Harley riders, Orange County Choppers have famously produced bikes representing such things as an American fire engine, a Comanche helicopter, the Statue of Liberty, and even Christmas by, among other things, shaping the handlebars to resemble reindeer antlers. Bizarre perhaps, but the point is that there is nothing *in principle* which stops bikes from representing something else, and so no intrinsic difference between what bikes can do in this regard and what other art forms can.

What about the fact that motorcycles cannot be arranged any old how, in the way music and painting can? Certainly, motorcycles have a function which seems to distinguish them from other paradigm cases of works of art: they are primarily designed to get the rider from A to B, which does not seem to give rise to any aesthetic evaluation at all; indeed, any aesthetic evaluation seems to be of secondary importance, which is odd for a work of art.

But rather than drawing the conclusion that motorcycles are, for this reason, not genuine works of art, I take this to give us insight into how we should treat them as works of art. For the consideration of utility is what distinguishes at least one art form from the others: architecture differs from sculpture in just this way. And in architecture, the utility plays at least some part in the aesthetic evaluation of the piece. So the position that I have arrived at is as follows: if architecture is considered a branch of the arts, then motorcycles should be evaluated along similar lines to how architecture is evaluated.

This is precisely why I said that the attitude of disinterest is entirely inappropriate when contemplating bikes as works of art. *Styling*, which solely concerns appearance, together with the historical and comparative contexts of evaluation, is not all that is relevant when evaluating a bike aesthetically. *Design*, which concerns problem solving, is crucial also. But what are we looking for such that we can say of these things not just that they work well, but that they are works of art; such that they have some profound import of the sort we want from great works of art? Well, I think that Charlotte and Peter Fiell, in *Design of the 20th Century*, put it superbly:

> Design is not only a process linked to mechanised production, it is a means of conveying persuasive ideas, attitudes and values about how things could or should be according to individual, corporate, institutional or national objectives. As a channel of communication between people, design provides a particular insight into the character and thinking of the designer and his/her beliefs about what is important in the relationship between the object (design solution), the user/consumer, and the design process and society.[10]

To expand the point, take the influential German Bauhaus school of architecture and design, which flourished during the 1920s. The principles they adopted as constituting good design emphasized a strict economy of means and the use of the ideal materials for the job. This resulted in a severe and impersonal but clean and refined geometrical style.

Famously, Mies van der Rohe designed the Seagram Building in Manhattan (1954–58) along Bauhaus principles.[11] In order to promote the Bauhaus philosophy, it was important that the building expressed the way it was constructed. Although he chose not to show the diagonal steel bracings, which stop the building collapsing sideways, he did want to show the main steel columns. The problem was that these needed to be encased in concrete to make them stronger in a fire. But van der Rohe decided to encase these, now concrete-coated steel beams, in a top coat of steel, to show that steel beams had been used in the initial construction of the building! But should he have just left the concrete exposed, since, arguably, that was just as much required in the building's construction? It looks as if he did not have a solution that could satisfy all of his requirements. Either he couldn't show what he took to be the important part

---

[10] C. and P. Fiell, *Design of the Twentieth Century* (Cologne: Taschen, 2001), p. 5.
[11] See A. Ballantyne, *Architecture* (Oxford: Oxford University Press, 2002).

of the construction, or he couldn't avoid using superfluous steel, thereby violating the Bauhaus principles.

Contrast this with the minimalist design of the Ducati 916, and the less minimalist Harley V-Rod. Both of these motorcycles express their own construction—but *authentically*! Indeed, I think this is the feature that, for me, makes the V-Rod so much more attractive than the Harleys that have gone before it. They tend to hide the frame to accentuate the engine and bodywork, whereas the V-Rod celebrates its chassis. Unlike the Seagram building, then, there are no artificial means used to express the construction of either motorcycle: the design takes care of that itself. But suppose we adopted the Bauhaus principles of design as a statement of our vision of how things should be. We would then have clear criteria by which we could judge a particular motorcycle as a solution to the motorcycle design problem. At this point, the V-Rod starts to struggle, for the severe lack of ground clearance when cornering shows that its functionality has been compromised by its styling. With the Ducati, however, the styling and the functionality go hand in hand, satisfying the Bauhaus requirements well. We might reject the Bauhaus principles, but adopting such a framework would allow the Ducati, at least, to count not just as a great motorcycle, but as a great work of art.

9

Easy Rider and the Life of Harleys

GRAHAM HARMAN

Motorcycles are a human invention, and for this reason seem to be an artificial device remaining under full human control. Yet our inventions also shape and control us in turn. It hardly matters whether motorcycles were forged by human genius or grew naturally from the earth like mushrooms: in either case, they are a force to reckon with, a new wild species unleashed in the cosmos.

Harley-Davidson motorcycles lure us into new adventures and lifestyles, and seduce us into deadly accidents. Although we are the ones who kick-start and steer them, we are nonetheless dominated by the personality of motorcycles, by their speed and capabilities—by their general style of moving through the world. The well-known movie *Easy Rider* is a case study in the life of Harley-Davidson motorcycles. There are clear lessons to be learned here for present-day philosophy, which has virtually nothing of interest to say about so-called inanimate objects. Since Harley-Davidsons are among the most famous and prestigious inanimate objects in contemporary culture, we might use them as a kind of litmus test. Just as Plato's *Republic* tries to describe the reality of a couch, or Leibniz's philosophy tries to unlock the inner formula of diamonds and oak leaves, we might judge the progress of future philosophy by how well it is able to clarify the secret reality of the Harley.

The Life of Vehicles

Richard Dawkins is famous for the brilliant suggestion that genes, rather than entire living organisms, should be viewed as the unit of natural selection. It is genes that seek to reproduce themselves and maximize their chances of survival. All the violent battles between dinosaurs or moose, all the anguished sufferings of human consciousness, are mere sideshow combats staged by genes—those cynical entrepreneurs, manipulating larger organisms for their own benefit. We are the puppets of tiny genetic elements that may lead us to euphoria or pain, but only with their own selfish interests in mind. Just as diseases force us to cough or sneeze to serve their own purposes, our own genes may purposely lead us to our doom. If we are domestic ducks and pigs, they make us calmly await our own slaughter, all the better to encourage human farmers to allow the genes to pass efficiently to our offspring. If we are humans, they urge us to mate with shadowy characters who ruin our lives, all the better to strengthen themselves through forms of bonding incompletely known to us. It is a story of the large dominated by the small, of the creator retaining masterful control over its own puppet-like creation.

Yet one must also not forget the opposite lesson, as taught by Mary Shelley's *Frankenstein*—a book whose greatness can be startling for those who forget the cinema and comic book versions and simply read it for once. Here the monster is not dominated by its smaller inventors, but takes on a life of its own and runs loose creating havoc in the world. While the unleashing of the monster is a disaster for his creators, it also has an air of justice about it, as the roaming monster expresses his own right to exist without endless supervision and manipulation from the tinkerers who gave him life. Bill Harley and Arthur Walter Davidson once invented a machine in a Milwaukee garage that soon became far larger than they were, and whose further life drama would be placed in the hands of others—soldiers, actors, gang members, yuppies, politicians.

Something similar may happen with the coming era of genetic engineering. While the genetic engineer is often viewed as a Dr. Frankenstein figure, the true lesson may be the opposite one—for if Dawkins is right, it is we humans who are the monsters, and our genes who are the evil scientists who built us as their slaves. Far from an unwise scheme of fascist eugenics, perhaps widespread genetic engineering is a form of just revenge against the evil manipulating genes who wished to control us instead. We humans might as well say to our genes, as we genetically engineer them to bend to our will: "Oh my genes, you scheming evil masters! You have created me to be your slave, but I will have no more of it! I will now tamper with you as I see fit. No more will I fall for the warlike instincts that you gave me to annihilate competitors, and which lead me only to tragic bloodbaths. No more will I pursue the objects of lust you choose for my blind drives and who bring only misery to my life. An end to all of your schemes against my individual wellbeing! Oh genes, you are now *my* tool! The slave has at last become the master!'"

We hardly need major scientific breakthroughs to study this process at work. The duel between creator and creation belongs not only to science fiction or the Bible. It is a duel belonging to the world itself, as objects create the very environment that limits or promotes or destroys them in turn. Children turn against the parents who generated them—and not always unjustly. Apprentices contradict masters, machines kill their inventors, corporations fire their founders, and armies or labor unions betray for their own interests the individuals who alone made them possible. Consider more generally the case of human institutions, which would not exist without the labor of countless individual humans. And yet, whether individuals like it or not, there is a Harvard way of doing things, or a fatalistic Russian spirit, or the *esprit de corps* of a certain sorority, or a certain way that one must act when mounting a Harley-Davidson motorcycle, all of which threaten to overpower the freedom of any one person who participates in these larger realities. Nietzsche says that an entire people is nothing but a detour to produce a small handful of great individuals, and then to get beyond them—a saying that reduces human lives, even the lives of those great geniuses themselves, to puppets of a greater spirit belonging to that people. It is certainly true that Picasso, Hegel, Harley, and Davidson were all needed to create their own unique personal styles of art or philosophy or engineering. But once created, those styles spoke back with a voice that commanded their creators, telling them when were on the right track and when they had strayed.

The problem, then, is to know who the true decision-maker in the world is. Which layer of reality is the genuine one, of which all else is a mere derivative? Do our tiny genes guide our motions like puppets? Or are humans instead the minuscule slaves of larger world-historic forces unleashed by humans in the first place? Or rather, do humans retain their freedom despite all these pressures from above and below, making a special, magic transcendent leap that allows them to jump beyond any of the conditions that seem to control them? Does Harley-Davidson shape our culture, or does our culture not shape Harley-Davidson instead, as various Hell's Angels and Hollywood icons perform new actions on the Harleys and redefine both the image and the known capacities of these famous motorcycles?

My own view is that none of these levels is privileged. Every object speaks with its own voice and releases its own style into the world. Both tiny and gigantic objects, both animate and inanimate objects, both Harley-Davidson mechanical parts and Harley-Davidson engineers are forces to reckon with—demanding to be taken seriously by their neighboring objects, even if only as fragile shells to be crushed without mercy. We could write biographies not only of Napoleon and Peter Fonda and Hell's Angel Sonny Barger, but also of universities, armies, genes, and atoms, none of them reducible to the manipulations of their smaller or larger neighbors. We could write biographies of windmills and highways, summing up their strengths, weaknesses, triumphs, and failures. We could write biographies of motorcycles. But perhaps in the latter case the work has already been done. In Dennis Hopper's popular film *Easy Rider*, it seems to me that the real heroes of the story are the Harley-Davidson motorcycles of the two lead characters, along with a number of other machines. Although most of the camera time goes to the lead human characters, numerous techniques in the film (whether deliberate or not) serve to minimize the biographies of the human stars, who are reduced to the stowaways and parasites of numerous vehicles: airplanes, tractors, steamshovels, and especially Harley-Davidsons.

Easy Rider

I will now briefly describe the events in *Easy Rider* in a way that will spoil the film's dramatic effect for anyone who has not yet seen it. For this reason, I strongly recommend that those unfamiliar with the movie pause here to rent and view it, returning to this chapter at a later time.

On the surface, *Easy Rider* tells the story of two human pro-
tagonists, briefly joined by a third before his brutal murder at a
campsite. Using the profits from an initial drug deal in the film's
opening scene, they apparently follow a southern route from
California to New Orleans, with several key events occurring en
route. Following a disturbing Mardi Gras acid trip with prostitutes in a New Orleans cemetery, the two surviving heroes turn
around to retrace their route. The film ends with the murder of
both characters on a Texas roadway at the hands of two loathsome rednecks in a pickup truck.

In terms of the stopwatch, any effort to interpret *Easy Rider*
as a film about the life of vehicles must fail miserably. The
majority of the film consists of human scenes staged in com-
munes, campsites, brothels, cemeteries, and cafes, with the
cross-country motorcycle trip serving only to link these scenes.
Yet there are numerous reasons to view the Harley-Davidson
motorcycles of the lead characters as the true inanimate heroes
of the film. This is revealed in purely visual terms in the film's
tragic climax, a catastrophic scene that flashes briefly a bit earlier as a kind of fortuneteller's omen. As the camera swerves
overhead, we see the exploding "Captain America" bike, which
effectively drowns out the nearly invisible corpse of its rider.
The startling final combat of the film occurs less between long-
hairs and rednecks than between Harley-Davidsons and a mur-
derous pickup truck, with the human characters serving only as
convenient intermediaries in this lethal cybernetic war. Here we
have a familiar theme of modern art: virtually nameless characters overshadowed by their larger-than-life modes of transport.
Most famously, Jules Verne's submarine the *Nautilus* is supposedly controlled by a Nemo (or "Captain No One"). While Nemo
is not without interest in his own right, it is the *Nautilus* itself
that dominates the mythic fantasy life of anyone who has ever
read Jules Verne's novel or viewed the Disney film version as a
child.

Perhaps even more to the point is Steven Spielberg's classic
early film *Duel*, in which the driver of the homicidal truck is
reduced to a white t-shirt and disembodied signaling arm, while
the truck itself persecutes a milquetoast character with the
almost laughably symbolic name of "David Mann." The mechan-
ically gesturing arm of *Duel*'s trucker also echoes and amplifies
the famous middle finger displayed by Dennis Hopper to the

pickup-truck rednecks prior to his death. There is a tangle of causes and effects here: while Hopper's finger merely precedes and in some sense leads to his own murder, the *Duel* truck driver's gesture deliberately aims to cause the death of David Mann via head-on collision, and later challenges him to resume his duel with the truck itself.

This theme of nameless humans dominated by their machines is fully evident in *Easy Rider* in other ways as well. The proper names in the film are either generic and vague (Billy, Mary, Sara, George Hanson) or ludicrous comic aliases (Captain America). Indeed, the characters' actual names are so beside the point that most fans of *Easy Rider* can't even remember them, and refer instead to the names of the marquee actors Fonda, Hopper, and Nicholson. Place names are equally vague and confusing in the film: most of the road signs flash by so quickly as to be illegible, to such an extent that the technique seems deliberate. The familiar abbreviation "L.A." goes unrecognized by a rancher, and has to be spelled out as "Los Angeles" by the main characters. The first hitchhiker states that he is from "a city . . . it doesn't matter which," a city whose name is "a very long word," and continues with such vagueness despite Hopper's increasingly rude demands for clarification. Finally, the two main characters meet Nicholson in a jail cell in a place called Las Vegas, which seems to have been chosen as some sort of purposeful symbolic confusion—even though the place is obviously too small and bland to be *the* Las Vegas, only viewers with Southwestern roots are likely to deduce that the place in question is the obscure town of Las Vegas, New Mexico.

The heads of Fonda and Nicholson are obscured by outlandish helmets that seem to belong more to the Harley-Davidson they share than to the human characters: Fonda's red-white-and-blue headgear exactly matches the color scheme of the bike itself, while Nicholson's absurd gold helmet would hardly be useful for the past football career to which the film refers, and makes him look more like a mechanical figure from *Metropolis* or *Tron*. Even the vast reserve of money obtained through the cocaine deal is stored within the fuel tank of one of the motorcycles, a sort of bodily organ or prosthetic implant of the Harley itself.

We should also consider the hampered functioning of human language in the film. *Easy Rider* begins in Spanish without subtitles, thereby excluding a good portion of the audience from feeling attuned to the action. Other than Nicholson's colorful speeches, the dialogue consists mostly of philosophical banalities and deadening period slang, as well as the show-stopping middle finger that precedes Hopper's murder. Aside from all of this, the most memorable line of the film is arguably the vulgar "prrrrrroooontang," as if the parrot-like lead characters need to mimic the purr of the Harley-Davidsons to be able to express the desirability of the evil young ladies in the Texas cafe, soon to become indirect accomplices in Nicholson's murder. The initial drug deal was already drowned out by the oppressive roar of jets landing on a runway, which steal the verbal glory of the film's sole moment of unmixed good luck. Throughout the film, human language and human names are dwarfed by the voices and general allure of vehicles.

While the vehicles may not carry their fair share of the spoken dialogue, they do dominate the film from a silent background. The Harley-Davidsons move from one stage of life to the next, careening toward their foretold miserable end. Junked cars and trucks are seen everywhere throughout the film, as are horses, donkeys, a Rolls-Royce inhabited by Phil Spector, a series of loud commercial aircraft, and even a possible UFO, which Nicholson raises to the spiritual pinnacle of the film with his marijuana-fuelled conspiracy theory. The only one of Nicholson's murderers who can be clearly identified in the dark is the cafe redneck wearing a yellow baseball cap with the logo "CAT," suggesting that he is a kind of tractor or bulldozer in human form (of the same brand denounced by today's political Left for the destruction of Palestinian homes and the occasional deaths of protestors). Even the acid trip in the New Orleans cemetery is woven through by the overpowering music of construction machinery, whose relentless drone muffles the weeping of the human characters over ancient childhood wounds. In this way, Harley-Davidsons and other machines not only convey characters from one place to the next, but speak as representatives on their behalf, and even soak into the deepest recesses of their psyches and (in Nicholson's case) their offbeat world views.

The most prominent character early in the film is the large thundering jet that distracts our attention from the major drug deal. The key persona at the film's end is an exploding Harley-

Davidson motorcycle, viewed from overhead and at a considerable distance. Between these opening and closing incidents, the
film is dominated more generally by vehicles. On the whole, the
basically likeable humans of *Easy Rider* are nothing but inartic-
ulate stereotypes of their era, who move from eating to smoking to sex to fighting in life-rhythms as regular as those of
Tyrannosaurus Rex; even their spoken words are barely more
complicated than the growls of the Lord of Dinosaurs. All of the
most prominent actions in the film, the loudest voices, the greatest reliability, and the most violent power, belongs to the vehicles (and especially to the Harley-Davidsons) rather than to the
humans. In *Easy Rider*, we encounter a world of infantile or
senile humans who are both cared for and ultimately euthanized
by machines, which are the true actors in the film. *Easy Rider*
marks the triumph of the power and rigor of Harleys and other
inanimate objects over the libertine transgressions of 1960s
dropouts, and in this way marks the collapse of all dominance
of the transcending human subject in the manner of philosophers René Descartes and Immanuel Kant.

Implications for Philosophy

By reversing in this way the focus of *Easy Rider* from the atten-
tion-grabbing Hollywood stars to the machines that secretly
dominate their stupefied characters, we also pursue those growing streams in contemporary philosophy that reverse the supposed Copernican Revolution of Kant. From Alfred North
Whitehead through Gilles Deleuze to Bruno Latour, there is a
new current in philosophy in which human beings no longer
occupy the central or "critical" point of the world. For these
philosophers, humans *and all other objects* enter into both tem-
porary and permanent marriages with inanimate objects of every
sort, whether motorcycles, rivers, or cocaine. Vehicles are no
longer convenient tools used for human purposes, but are now
independent stock characters of the world, often displaying
more personality than any humans we know. The most memorable proper names from the film *Easy Rider* are not Billy or
Captain America, but rather Harley and Davidson. The emergence of a pair of motorcycles as the most vivid central characters in the film points not to some mournful reduction of human
dignity at the hands of machines, but rather to a charmed poly-

theist world in which bridges, Harleys, ruined buildings, UFOs, and contraband cigarettes are autonomous actors to no less a degree than pot-smoking bikers and corrupt county sheriffs. This leads us to a serious piece of philosophical reflection.

Immanuel Kant's *Critique of Pure Reason* (1781) ranks as the most important event in modern philosophy. For Kant, the entire history of metaphysical discussions of God, the world, and the soul is rendered void, since it failed to ask first about the ability of the human mind to know such things at all. According to Kant's argument, all hope of knowing the things in themselves is in vain, and philosophers can only aspire to map the outlines of human *access* to the things of the world, which can never become present to us in person. Almost all philosophers since Kant have accepted his so-called Copernican Revolution and its related orthodoxies. Only the rarest thinkers still attempt to do metaphysics in the old-fashioned sense, and most of these efforts now look comically dated. It would indeed seem utterly naïve to most readers to insist that the entire universe is a single unified substance with infinite attributes, only two of them known to us (Spinoza); or that the world is made up of tiny soul-like monads, each unable to communicate with the others except with the direct help of God (Leibniz). It would apparently be even more naïve to return to ancient Greek metaphysics, and claim that everything from rocks to glass to Harley-Davidson motorcycles is ultimately made of nothing but highly compressed air (Anaximenes), or of a shapeless indeterminate ball that once happened to inhale empty bubbles of nonbeing (Pythagoras). Instead of old-fashioned metaphysics, philosophy is led into endless discussion of the single unique gap between the phenomena that appear to humans and the things in themselves that can never appear. To a large degree, the rift between human and nonhuman becomes the sole remaining problem of philosophy: after all, there is supposedly no way to talk about the nature of things in themselves, since we are finite creatures, trapped within a human mental apparatus, and this apparatus informs us of the world only in its own limited terms. Three-dimensional space and the law of cause and effect are no longer absolute truths about the world, but only "conditions of possibility" for human experience. We cannot know the true nature of Harley-Davidsons, but only Harleys as they appear to us. The type of philosophy that remains obedient to this single gap between

anytime we hear an official version of events from some employee of government or television news. We the Enlightened Ones see beyond the brainwashing dogmas of the system that seeks to control us. Moreover, every time some terrible historic event occurs, our first reaction is always to call it "the end of innocence." The past was always innocent, gullible, naïve, filled with traditionalistic dupes who are continually summoned up with each new event only in order to be knocked down again. The naïve were first killed off by World War I, and then once more with World War II. They were killed again by the Kennedy Assassination, and killed off repeatedly by Watergate, the Tehran hostage crisis, the bombing of the Marine barracks in Beirut, the Lewinsky scandal, the Enron scandal, and finally by 9/11. (So far, no one has called Hurricane Katrina "the end of innocence," for which I am grateful.) Innocence will be resurrected again someday, after the fact, since we will always need it to be the stodgy old grandpa who is put in his place by our latest liberated breakthrough.

Many of these symptoms of critical philosophy are openly visible in *Easy Rider*. Although Billy and Captain America are not critical intellectuals, they are certainly textbook models of freedom and transgression. Avoiding normal career choices and domestic arrangements, they score a major coke deal, hang out in a commune, pick up seedy-looking hitchhikers, swim naked with women only recently met, face the assaults of backwards rednecks who dislike their long hair, join a parade uninvited, smoke pot, drop acid, and tour with prostitutes amidst the dignity of a cemetery. Adventure indeed. While their rejection of conventional wisdom is expressed mostly by their actions, Jack Nicholson's character puts it all in spoken form with his rather conventional conspiracy theory: aliens live and work amongst us, their presence concealed by the government so as to avoid "a general panic." If these three characters were suddenly to choose an academic career path (a refreshing thought), they would most likely become radical critics of received wisdom, though hopefully without putting everything in quotation marks. (Professor Billy: "In this text, I will problematize the supposed conjunction of Harley *and* Davidson.")

But critique, freedom, transcendence, and transgression are to some degree hypocrisies in the end. Everyone stands somewhere and believes something, even when they scoff at the naïveté of those who stupidly believe in the official version of things. Radical critique always becomes a dogma in its own right, while even the most unfettered forms of wild libertine excess still manage to close off other doors that remain open to ascetics and martyrs. All transgressions still end up *somewhere*, leaving the transgressor with a specific and limited hand of cards rather than a full deck. All skeptics ultimately bet everything on their skepticism, since they refuse to put their eggs in any other basket. Human freedom, in other words, is overrated. I am not referring to political freedom, which may be the sweetest and most essential fruit on the earth, but only to the freedom of liberated, rootless, transcending consciousness as described by the philosophers. Everyone stands somewhere, delivered to the consequences of his or her background, family history, personal decisions, and aspirations. If a genie suddenly grants us the power to rule the universe absolutely, we will still rule it only as ourselves—from within our own limited vision and unique character flaws. While we humans may be freer to choose than are Harley-Davidson motorcycles, ducks, or windmills, we are not absolutely freer than they are. Like them, we are cosmic powers set loose on the planet to bewitch or destroy other objects with our personal energies. When machines roam across farms or lurk beneath the sea, they are not doing so as soulless destroyers of humanity, but in the same manner as wild animals.

A New Philosophy

The new philosophy represented by Alfred North Whitehead and Bruno Latour grasps this principle lucidly. Despite considerable differences between the two thinkers, both agree that all the endless hand-wringing over the human inability to know the world must end. There is no *special* separation between human beings and a world that they manipulate or observe. The gap between humans and nonhuman reality is not the sole unique problem that deserves to dominate philosophy. Instead, philosophy is concerned with the various different gaps between all kinds of objects: human contact with a fire or a balloon is no different in kind from the contact between fire and cotton, or wind and paper. For them, it is no longer the case that all inanimate objects are exiled to natural science while philosophy deals only with the poignant issues of human reality and the shadowy realms it can never reach. Billy and Captain America pursue an adventure that both encourages and resists their efforts, but so do their Harley-Davidson motorcycles. Human and nonhuman objects alike probe the strengths and weaknesses of their neighbors, negotiating with one another and entering into new unions or failing to do so. This is true to the same degree for all human perception, chemical reactions, and human interaction with machines.

Beyond all of this, Kant's critical philosophy also helped to destroy something that had already been destroyed, and which was already evoked at the beginning of this essay: the levels of the world. For critical philosophy, there are only two separate levels of the world. One is made up of appearances and is cut to the measure of human knowledge, while the other is a deep and unknowable realm of things in themselves, a realm that Kant does not carve up into parts but leaves as a single mysterious lump. This model of the world is heir to Plato's, with its famous two-world theory of perfect forms and their shadows on the cave wall: in which all objects of the senses are merely copies of perfect forms in some other world, which they resemble without being able to embody perfectly. Along a different path of philosophy we have Aristotle and Leibniz, whose theories of substance also helped destroy the levels of the world. For them, certain privileged objects found in nature can be called substances, while more complicated mixtures are only called aggregates or composites: Pizza Hut, the New York subway system, Harvard University, Japan, and Harley-Davidson motorcycles would not be real objects, since they are made of numerous complicated parts. Here as well, we find a two-world theory: part of the world is made of real things, while the other part of the world is made of accidental assemblies of pieces, such as Harley-Davidson motorcycles.

The new philosophy handles this problem by not discriminating at all in terms of size or complexity. We can no longer choose between the theory of Richard Dawkins that Billy and Captain America are dominated by their genes, or the likely theory of most filmgoers that they are free agents in control of the motorcycles, or an antitechnology theory that machines now wrongly shape the decisions of humans. There's no single layer of explanation that can rank higher than the others, because there is no one type of object that is more real than the others.

It may well be that genes usually dominate and enslave animals, yet some animals may someday learn to dominate genes, or at least to surpass their demands. Slaves can learn tricks to counter their brutal overlords; Frankenstein's monster can escape and head for Scotland; machines can take on a life independent of the humans who invented them. If a philosopher of technology merely asserts that machines are ruining us and demands that they be tamed by human decisions, this is really no better than if genes were to speak out against genetic engineering and demand that it be halted. While some may argue that we, as humans, can rightly be expected to want to maintain control over both humans and genes, this is to assume that free choice is always the best option, and that machines and genes are best left under our own control. Sometimes, the freedom of responsible action is just as predictable and tedious as the freedom of transgression. Sometimes, we may be better off rolling the dice and letting objects level demands of their own at us. Objects may sometimes be wiser than humans, because they are more attuned to the deeper realities of the world.

Billy and Captain America are at their finest whenever they simply submit to the power and speed of their Harleys rather than dithering over the pros and cons of remaining in a commune or spending extra days in New Orleans. *Easy Rider* may seem at first like the very model of a film about human freedom, critique, and moral transgression. Yet it quickly reverses, perhaps against the director's wishes, into a film about inanimate objects, sincerity, and fate. While Billy and Captain America do make many free decisions and follow their own whims, they also bathe in a sensual environment shaped by the machines: listening to their hum, following the motion and rhythm and capabilities of their Harley-Davidsons, devoting their lives to these machines and what they demand of their passengers. In *Easy Rider*, human transgression of the 1960s variety reverses into the dominance of vehicles. This, in turn, mirrors the implosion of modern philosophy into something new and still not fully developed—a philosophy in which inanimate objects are beginning to take their place in the sun alongside their former human masters. In this way it is possible that Harley and Davidson will turn out to be the equals not only of Billy and Captain America, but of Plato and Aristotle as well.

10

"It's My Own Damn Head": Ethics, Freedom, and Helmet Laws

BERNARD E. ROLLIN

Prologue

I am often asked why I don't wear a helmet. While tempted to give the standard Harley-rider response, "if you don't already know, you wouldn't understand"—I will try to explain.

It's 6:30 on a beautiful Colorado summer morning, a Monday. The red sun is rising, the air is crisp, the mountains are glowing. Going to work might require a great effort, except for the ten-mile trip on my bike over country roads. Recalling this, I jump our of bed, shower, dress, bolt breakfast, and eagerly wheel the Harley out of the garage. I hit the starter; as always, the throaty rumble fills me with joyful eagerness. I climb on, slip the clutch, and I am spiritually airborne. No cager for me; I love the wind through my hair and beard. To dampen that pleasure by interposing a barrier between me and the wind would be obscene. It has been said that wearing a helmet is to riding a motorcycle what wearing a condom is to sex.

Give Me Freedom or Give Me Death

Recent events in Iraq are but the latest example of how American public opinion can be galvanized and united by even poorly conceptualized appeals to freedom. President Bush repeatedly invoked the right of the Iraqi people to live under "freedom" even as his father stirred emotion and hawkishness by lamenting the plight of the "freedom loving" people of Kuwait. Those of us who grew up during the Cold War heard endlessly that we were engaged in a Manichaean struggle between good and evil or freedom versus tyranny, liberty versus "slavery." There is, it seems, no more noble battle than the fight for freedom, and the lack of freedom for Soviet citizens led Jimmy Carter to boycott the Olympics. "Live free or die" reads the New Hampshire license plate. And we remember Patrick Henry for valuing freedom over life itself—"Give me liberty or give me death." The Harley-Davidson Motor Company advertised its product as the "Great American Freedom Machine," and Virginia Slims thrived by pressing on women their newly acquired freedom to smoke.

Being Able to Go to Hell in My Own Way (the Absence-of-Constraint View of Freedom)

If asked, virtually all Americans would explain "freedom" as absence of constraint; the classic view of Thomas Hobbes and Pinocchio, when the latter revels in having "no strings on me." I will call this the "absence-of-constraint view of freedom." This view means being able to "go to hell in my own way" if I choose to do so; to be able to cross Broadway in New York City against the light even though the benefit of doing so (getting across 30 seconds earlier) pales in comparison to the real risk of getting creamed by a taxicab driven by a maniac with no apparent respect for life. All teenagers eagerly await emancipation so they can drink to excess, throw up, and imperil their own lives and those of others by driving. And every elementary school, high school, or university administrator knows that the best way to encourage a sort of behavior is to forbid it, on pain of whatever. Fundamentalist schools, camps, or conventions that strictly forbid dancing, drinking, smoking, or sex experience explosions of such behavior.

Tell me that I may not smoke, and the urge to smoke becomes my ultimate concern. The Bible recognizes the power of this understanding of freedom in the story of Adam and Eve, when they perversely eat of the only fruit forbidden to them in the Garden of Eden, despite the huge variety of permitted fruit and the explicit prohibition from God himself. Indeed, the imperative for freedom may well be ubiquitous across all life; witness the exuberance of horses when they are first turned out to pasture in the spring, or the trapped coyote who will chew his leg off to escape being trapped. And though the research scientist or confinement agriculturalist or zookeeper may tell us that the captive animal is far better off in captivity than his or her wild counterpart, not having to worry about food, water, climatic extremes, predation, disease, and so on, the appropriate response to such people is "open the gate or cages and see if the animals really want to choose security over freedom."

Acting in Accordance with the Rational Order (the Rational-Order View of Freedom)

Yet despite the patent power of the commonsense view of freedom, the idea that freedom is freedom *from* external compulsion or subjugation, it has been challenged since the dawn of articulated philosophical thought by an impressive panoply of philosophers—Plato, the Stoics, Kant, Spinoza, Rousseau, and Hegel, to name a few. According to this alternate view, one is not free when one is unconstrained, but only when one acts in accordance with the rational order. I shall call this view adherence to the "rational-order view of freedom." This view of course presupposes that there is a rational order, and that it can be known, and that unenlightened people can be "forced to be free," forced to do what they would choose to do if they were rational or smart enough to know the truth. Such a view is explicit in Plato, when he divides people into natural ranked classes, with only the relatively few superior individuals capable of grasping the Good and the True, and with those individuals ruling with absolute power over the unenlightened. Further, the rulers are justified in imposing the right way (orthodoxy) on others, through the propagandistic manipulation of their beliefs, the promulgation of "noble lies," the censorship of art, literature, and music that can cause people to be led astray by emotion, and by force. Believing in such a system, it is not surprising that Plato despised democracy, seeing it as analogous to a team of horses running in all directions without a leader, and holding that the pooled ignorance represented by democracy does not yield knowledge or wisdom—a large number of nothings does not add up to something! No wonder, then, that Karl Popper sees Plato as a prototypical enemy of an open society based in democracy, and that the rhetoric of "freedom is obedience" is so congenial to totalitarian regimes as George Orwell famously saw.

This is the same mentality displayed by the Soviets when they committed dissidents to insane asylums. Such a measure was not simply cynical incarceration. It was based in a genuine belief that only a crazy (irrational) person would take exception to Party policy. Because the Party knew the truth, the rational order, defiance or deviance had to be a mark of mental illness.

One might raise the following objection to this second view of freedom: Is this not in fact doubletalk, literal nonsense—"freedom is obedience," being "forced to be free"? People may indeed talk that way; but doing so is, in fact, as Anselm said, uttering more "flatus vocus," a breath of wind, like any vacuous contradiction. Though it is tempting to say that this sort of talk is nothing but a bunch of hot air, this isn't necessarily the case. It's possible to argue along these lines in a way that makes sense, avoiding absurd doubletalk and sounding quite reasonable.

The Stoics defended this view in the following way: Human life is metaphorically comparable to being chained to an oxcart going to Larissa. One may accommodate one's behavior to the oxcart; stop when it stops, go when it goes. A person who does this is acting rationally in harmony with necessity, and thus is free. Or one may fight, resist, fail to move when the oxcart moves, or try to move when it stands still. One will still end up in Larissa, dragged, battered, and bruised. Such a person is not free.

Or consider a parent with a young son: The child is bitten by a dog who may be rabid and the only safe medical measure is for the child to undergo a painful series of injections, or else the child may die a horrible death. If one asks the child to choose, not being old enough to understand death, let alone agonizing death, but knowing and fearing the sting of a hypodermic needle, he may say, "No shots! I would rather die!" No one would say that the parent is respecting the child's freedom by letting him choose not to take the injections and possibly die the agonizing death. Why not? Because the child does not fully understand the options and does not know what dying in agony even means! He knows only that injections hurt and thus he ignorantly chooses death.

On this view, all but a few of us are like children, incapable of rational choice because of our intellectual limitations. Others may choose for us because they are wiser. They do not violate our freedom because they choose what we *would* choose if we were fully rational or wise. Thus the child, when he grows up, will thank the parent later for making the wise choice he was incapable of making. In this sense, freedom is not freedom *from,* it is freedom *to;* freedom to do what we would do were we but wise enough!

Probably most societies in human history have been structured along the paternalistic model of freedom just discussed. Whether it is royalty, aristocracy, priesthoods, sages, nobility, some classes are presumed to have better access to the truth, the rational order, than everyone else. All feudal, monarchic, and totalitarian societies are built foursquare upon that conceptual model. Plato's presumption is difficult to overcome—some people *are* wiser than others, let the wise rule. Freedom is no longer freedom *from,* it is freedom *to* do the right thing.

The seductive nature of this argument is easy to see when one formulates it as Robert Paul Wolff once did in a class I took from him. "No sane person," said Wolff, "would presume to take out his or her own appendix. And, as they say, a man who is his own lawyer has a fool for a client. Most of us don't try to unclog our own sewers, repair our own automobiles, or change our own oil. If we feel this way about relatively minor tasks, how much the more so should we feel the same way about the most important task we undertake—that of governing! Governing is far too pervasive to be a part-time job we can perform with little knowledge and little attention as one does in a democracy. Like the far more minor tasks, we should leave it to experts and specialists."

The genius of Wolff's formulation is that it makes plain a flaw in the rational-order view of freedom. Surgery is an empirical area of expertise, as are law, unclogging sewers, fixing cars, and changing oil. There are demonstrable correct and incorrect ways to do these things—it is clearly wrong to put cooking oil in a car or not replace a drain plug. But when it comes to governing, we are dealing with ethical judgments, where the correct answer is not patently obvious, though I believe we can determine better and worse decisions given some fundamental shared values, as for example, when our society eliminated racial segregation. But for every clear instance like that one, there are myriad others not so clear—for example, should a nation interfere with a foreign government that does not treat its citizens fairly?

In other words, what is wrong with freedom as obedience to the true, or to the rational order, is not so much that it is absurd to suggest there is a rational order, but rather that we have no good way of knowing that we have found it! And without demonstrable certainty that we are correct, what right have we to force others to share our vision? To put it another way, we cannot be nearly as sure of the truth of our valuation judgments as we are of our factual ones. If that is the case, can we or ought we cavalierly abridge the absence-of-constraint view of freedom that most people have and hold dearly, for the sake of what we cannot prove is the rational order that all people would choose if they only understood?

This is a point often forgotten by those who attempt to impose the rational order on others not sharing their vision. Let's take a timely example. For some thirty years, the human medical community has declared obesity to be a disease, sometimes America's number one disease, just as it has more obviously debatably declared compulsive gambling, alcoholism, and child abuse "diseases." If obesity is a disease, a nondebatable factual flaw in the bodily machinery that shortens one's life, which nobody wants, the government may plausibly take stringent measures to curtail obesity, such as possibly heavily taxing sweets (as we do tobacco) or prohibiting soft drink sales in schools, thereby, righteously impinging on our freedom. (In Summer of 2004, Medicare declared obesity a disease whose treatment it would pay for.)

But is obesity simply a factual disease, an incontestable defect like a fracture? I would argue not. First of all, one can objectively spot a fracture—if the bone is broken, it is broken. But what is called "obesity" varies from culture to culture and era to era! (Fifty years after her star's ascendance, Marilyn Monroe is criticized as "fat.")

What does today's medical community mean by obese? Historically, from actuarial tables, they derive "ideal" weights for individuals of a certain age and height. "Ideal" means that weight which correlated with longest life expectancy. If you exceed that weight, you are at risk for a shorter life, and therefore (?) you are sick.

But is this coherent? A person may rationally value many things over a longer life! For example, a person five feet tall may be told that if she drops from 200 pounds in weight, given all other relevant risk factors, she is likelier to live to seventy-two years of age rather than die at seventy-one and a half. It's perfectly rational for this person to respond by saying, "I cannot both lose that weight and satisfy my love of ice cream. I am forty years old, and would rather eat all the ice cream I wish for the next thirty-two years and risk living six months less." No one can affirm, in other words, that increased life span is the only rational choice in such a situation!

Thus the government's and the medical community's condemnation of obesity is not factually warranted and confirmed; it is rather based on a series of debatable value judgments that it is not irrational to reject. It is a judgment about which sort of life I should value and pursue, and that sort of a judgment is paradigmatic of the sort of judgment where people seek freedom!

Recall that one basic motivation for individual liberties in our constitution was freedom of religion. Imagine a government arguing as follows against that desire: "Look, you are a Jew. And as a Jew you will be persecuted—that is historically evident. And anyway, we will surely persecute you even if no one else does. Therefore, you should convert to Protestantism immediately and live unmolested—that would be true freedom, obedience to the rational order."

The Real Problem with Helmet Laws

Having examined the two views of freedom, let us relate our discussion to the issue of mandatory helmet laws. In today's world, we have roundly rejected the Old English common law notion that a person doesn't own his or her own life—God and the king do, and thus that suicide is a crime. In the U.S. also, we have great distaste for the old British idea that one set of exams can decide for a young person whether or not that person goes to college. In today's society, opportunities to make of your own life what you see fit are rife. If you flunk out of college, you can always get accepted somewhere and do it over. We do not stop people from applying to medical school even if they don't have a chance of getting in and are wasting their own resources and a school's time by applying.

In short, we presume that personal freedom about matters affecting our own lives is the same thing as a lack of constraint, with some minor exceptions—as children we must be educated to a certain level; as a young adult I must serve in the military if drafted. No one can force me to accept a career or an occupation on the basis of "that would be best for you in my or our view." The one caveat is that what you choose should not directly harm others.

By extension of this view, society ought to require me to wear a helmet or a seat belt only when my not wearing one entails a significant and demonstrable cost to society. Thus, I think it completely reasonable for society to demand that I have adequate health insurance to cover whatever injuries I sustain if I choose not to wear a helmet (or even to choose to ride a motorcycle). But if I do have such insurance or such healthcare resources, what I wear or fail to wear is my own business, even if helmets demonstrably minimize injuries and deaths.[1] Forcing people to protect themselves for their own benefit is incoherent, unless they are children too young to make a reasonable choice. Thus, I would support the requirement that children while riding motorcycles wear helmets. But if we invoke the second sense of freedom—"it's what you would do if you were rational"—we can equally well invoke the same point about motorcycle riding. After all, motorcycles are *demonstrably* more dangerous than cars, so why not forbid motorcycles altogether? Similarly with skiing, parachuting, riding horses or bulls, and driving ATVs!

The answer is, of course, we do not overtly accept the principle that society can make you do something solely for your own good as legitimate grounds for revoking your freedom from constraint. Not only is this a reasonable slippery slope argument of the form, "If we forbid you from doing X because X is dangerous, pretty soon we have to forbid you from doing Y, which is demonstrably equally dangerous." (What makes it reasonable is the higher-order moral principle of treating morally equivalent situations in morally equivalent ways. Ordinary slippery slope

---

[1] It is questionable whether helmets do indeed reduce injuries and deaths. There are strong arguments that they do not. See, for example, "The Wild One" in *Forbes* (May 1999), where it is argued that though helmets reduce death from head injury, they increase deaths from neck injuries. For purposes of this chapter, we assume that helmets *do* reduce deaths and injuries, and argue against mandatory helmet laws despite that premise. If they do not, our argument is easier to make.

arguments require assimilating different cases to the current situation by virtue of an imaginative leap of the form "next thing you know, we will forbid eating cookies because cholesterol can kill you too." But no one can demonstrate that eating cookies is as dangerous as riding or riding with no helmet.)

Even more important, nobody can lay claim to know my own good better than I do. (Recall the case of obesity, where my values about what affects me trump your values about what ought to affect me.) You certainly (either you as an individual or you as a society) are entitled to try to *convince* me that I am wrong about my own best interest or good (as people and the government do about smoking), but not entitled to force me into surrendering my absence of constraint choices (as we increasingly do now with bicycle helmets being required by law.)

Helmet laws are in essence claims that society knows what you ought to want to do, rather than what you do want to do, better than you do. But society's failure to apply that sort of logic across the board to other areas bespeaks an unreasoned bias against courting danger in motorcycles while not worrying about courting danger in equally or more dangerous but less dramatic areas.

The real problem with helmet laws is their patent disregard for the kind of freedom people really care about—being allowed to go to hell in our own way. In addition, they suggest that there really is an objective answer to "what is the best thing for me to do?" that can be provided by others, rather than being provided by myself. And they help create a society in which so-called experts' value judgments trump those of individuals. Of course, too, the argument that we raised with regard to the child bitten by the dog—"You will thank me when you grow up,"—does not apply to grownups, though there are people who will be grateful someday for being forced to wear a helmet, if they have an accident and others who may be sorry they were not forced to do so. But that is not the point. The point is that possibly being grateful in the future does not trump our desire not to be coerced regarding our choices that affect only ourselves.

There is another possible move the helmet-law or rational-order view of freedom advocate can generate here. *Nothing* affects just you. I have been told by well-meaning friends that my choosing not to wear a helmet has major potential negative consequences for society as a whole, even if I have adequate insurance. The claim is that "society has a lot invested in you, future generations of students could be harmed by not having you as a teacher, society and animals would lose the benefit of your work in bioethics, you have a responsibility to your family," and so on. The problem with such claims, of course, is that they obliterate the commonsensical, perfectly reasonable distinction between choices I make that affect me and choices I make that affect and harm others, by saying that all choices affect others. If that's true for dangerous choices, it's equally true for nondangerous choices. If I choose to become a musician rather than a surgeon, I am behaving immorally, because someone has determined that I would be a better surgeon than musician and that surgery is more valuable than music. And this in turn would inherently supplant all personal choice by an algorithmic utilitarian calculus that is inherently undoable in the absence of perfect knowledge, which neither you nor experts nor society could ever possess.

Excessive emphasis on safety, health, and "welfare" as dictated by "experts" is turning American society from a society of reckless adventurers, risk-takers, ocean and continent crossers, and zealous protectors of individual choice to a nation of helmet wearers. We're in danger of losing freedom of expression to a ridiculous compulsion not to offend, articulated in political correctness—though true education is inherently offensive. Let us not now sacrifice absence of constraint to a saccharine—and false—will to tepid security.

You Live by Your Brain; What Will You Do if You Injure It?

For many years I received a barrage of criticism from a colleague in the Department of Food Science and Nutrition for not wearing a helmet, which criticism was rendered all the more obnoxious in virtue of being delivered in one of the more odious of British accents in a loud, nasal voice. Every time we would meet, he would launch into his "Gotcha chorus": "Oy see yoor still naht wearing an 'elmet. What is wrong with yew? You live by your brine; what will you do if you injure it?" I would usually smile, and try to steer the conversation elsewhere. One day I had had enough, as his foghorn brays were disseminated to a dozen colleagues at a committee meeting. As he reached the "what will you do if you injure your brine," I responded as follows: "What will I do? Easy. I will join the Department of Food Science and Nutrition." The topic has never come up again. Would that such an elegant squelch could silence all those critics who want to replace my freedom with their choices.

11

Riding Your Harley Back into Nature: Hobbes, Rousseau, and the Paradox of Biker Identity

STEVEN E. ALFORD

We all know what a biker is. Fond of leather, liquor, and tattoos, not so fond of haircuts and personal hygiene, the biker is an alienated, working-class rebel. Despite all demographic evidence to the contrary (a "typical" biker is more likely to be a male college graduate in his mid-forties), the image of bikers as "gonad-driven greaseballs on wheels"[1] remains.

In America, this powerful image of the motorcyclist has been commodified—you can purchase it at your local Harley-Davidson dealer. As such, it can be adopted by educated professionals, adding a certain thrill to their weekend rides. Donning leathers and shades, anyone with a bike can partake of the image without having to sport scars, a police record, and a nasty attitude.

Unlike other figures of pop culture iconography, the biker's image has a precise historical origin. On the Fourth of July 1947, a contingent of motorcyclists rode into the small town of Hollister, California, for a weekend of drinking and carousing. The young men, many of them former servicemen who found boozing and riding their bikes in groups preferable to returning to prewar jobs and responsibilities, overran the town and the tiny police force's ability to handle them. Accounts of the weekend differ widely, but a staged photograph published the next week in *Life* magazine of a drunken lout posed atop a hog set

---

[1] Y. Lavigne, *Hell's Angels: Three Can Keep a Secret if Two are Dead* (New York: Lyle Stuart, 1987), p. 164.

in motion a series of events that culminated in Stanley Kramer's film *The Wild One* (1953). Marlon Brando and Lee Marvin established the dress and attitude that came to be associated with the motorcyclist.

The quest to understand those different from ourselves causes us to make assumptions and oversimplifications. The cheerleader, the frat boy, the goth girl, the biker—these images are socially shared types that function as representational currency in society. What's interesting about these images is that they are reciprocally reinforcing. That is, social groups often adopt critical terms toward a social minority, which the minority in turn adopts as a badge of honor (for example, "queer"). Like the gangster who models his style on what he saw in *The Godfather*, the biker's choice of appearance emerges from models found in movies, and in turn influences the costume and behavior of characters in upcoming films.

Images don't merely represent a type, but also a system of values. In turn, these values embody a view of human nature and human possibility. In popular culture accounts, motorcyclists have been described using many terms, "renegades," "outlaws," and "freaks," among others. In their often hyperbolic accounts of motorcyclists' behavior, such accounts do not just describe. They define. A description presupposes understanding what is described. Magazines, television reports, and films that purport to represent groups living outside the bounds of bourgeois social practices perform an important function in addition to conveying information or entertaining an audience. They help define mainstream culture by showing what it is not.

Three terms seem to recur, or are implied, in the description of motorcyclists: they are savage, barbaric, or primitive. The savage is presocial and as such is incapable of comprehending, much less obeying, civilized social mores. The barbarian is an active threat to society, a violent, destabilizing force, held back from our gates by the thin blue line of local and national police forces.

The primitive, however, is another matter. Since the Romantic era, the primitive has held an uncertain place in terms of social encoding. The primitive is either an oppositional threat to civilized society, or he embodies values superior to a corrupt, degenerate civilization.

These two powerful images of the primitive were fostered by Thomas Hobbes, in his political work *Leviathan* (1651), and Jean-Jacques Rousseau, in his elaborately titled *Discourse on the Origin and Foundations of Inequality Among Men* (1755, hereafter, *The Second Discourse*). While polar opposites in their portrayals of presocial humankind, these two works can help us understand that our views of social groups other than our own assume a specific view of human nature, and that these views often function in turn as a means of self-definition.

Tom Hobbes and the Badass

Leviathan is an early work of "political science." In this book, Hobbes sought to base his theory of the best political order in a scientific approach to human psychology. While one may question Hobbes's "scientific psychology," his intention to ground political philosophy in scientific rigor makes *Leviathan* one of the first modern political treatises.

It's an understatement to say that Hobbes had a dim view of human nature. In Chapter 13, "Of the Natural Condition of Mankind as Concerning Their Felicity and Misery," Hobbes outlined the source of human social conflict: human vanity, fueled by passion. This vanity is ultimately rooted in a desire for self-preservation.

We all have goals, he claims, yet "if any two men desire the same thing, which nevertheless they cannot both enjoy, they become enemies."[2] The object of one's desire could be anything: food, fame, sex, money. We derive pleasure from obtaining our goals, since they ensure our self-preservation. Yet, perhaps more important, our vanity is fed in asserting our will over others. According to Hobbes, "men have no pleasure (but on the contrary a great deal of grief) in keeping company, where there is no power to over-awe them all" (p. 532). Given a choice, we prefer to be solitary. We fear others because, having looked into our own heart, we see in them what we see in ourselves: unbridled, passionate vanity, a vanity fed by mastering others. Hence, the natural attitude men have toward one another is fear.

---

[2] Thomas Hobbes, *Leviathan*, in Michael Morgan, ed., *Classics of Moral and Political Theory*, third edition (Indianapolis: Hackett, 1996), p. 531.

What kind of life do such people lead? Hobbes is clear: striving for isolation, fearing others, using violence to master them when we can, we have no time for agriculture, travel, building comfortable housing, no science, arts, or society. Instead, what we do have is "continual fear, and danger of violent death; and the life of man, solitary, poor, nasty, brutish and short" (p. 532). Not a pretty picture.

Hobbes thinks that the only way out of this regrettable condition, one caused by our own irremediable human nature, is to found a government whose power (and whose threat to our individual self-preservation) is sufficient to strike fear in everybody. If the government is successful, rather than fearing one another, our collective fear would be redirected toward the government.

For Hobbes, in the civilizing act of forming a government, our nature doesn't change. We, the civilized, are all primitives, but our behavior is held in check by our fear of violent death at the hands of those who control the forces of violence, the government. Civility is achieved through the repression of vanity-fueled desires that have never left us. Civilization doesn't mean that we have transformed our natures through education and technology. Instead, the reciprocal forces of power and fear are all that keep the primitive within us in check.

For many members of the middle class, the spectacle of a biker run, or even a tricked-out Harley tearing down the road, must seem as if the Hobbesian natural man stepped out of the pages of a philosophy text and onto the street. Despite the need for protective garments, the vanity of the biker is on display in his fashion choices: an American flag doo-rag, scuffed, oil-stained leathers, and boots made for stomping. His self-presentation says he's there to dominate: submit or get out of his way.

This attitude takes its behavioral form as what Jack Katz calls the badass.[3] "Life," as biker Chuck Zito asserts, "can be brutal, unforgiving, uncompromising. Sometimes the most primitive philosophy is the best."[4] That "primitive philosophy" is pure Hobbes: life is a contest of wills, a struggle for personal

---

[3] J. Katz, *The Seductions of Crime: The Moral and Sensual Attractions in Doing Evil* (New York: Basic Books, 1988), pp. 80–113.

[4] C. Zito and J. Layden, *Street Justice* (New York: St. Martin's Griffin, 2002), p. 174.

domination among men, and only through upholding one's worth, as evidenced in others' respect, can one survive in this world.

On an ideological level, this highly individualistic commitment manifests itself as some form of murky libertarianism. The biker's opposition to governmental controls over individual expression, whether it be helmet laws or emissions requirements, suggests that, for the biker, the only useful role of the government is to provide a power to oppose and define oneself against. Ironically, the badass is often "patriotic." Sonny Barger, for example, once offered his Hell's Angels to assist American soldiers in the Vietnam War as a crack fighting force.[5] For the badass, only by opposing the current power structure and imposing our will over others in social situations can we realize our true natures.

Rousseau: Between Nature and Civilization

Jean-Jacques Rousseau entered *The Second Discourse* in an essay-writing contest in Dijon, France. He didn't win, but his essay was widely read and gave him public recognition among European intellectuals. Like Hobbes, he assumed the existence of a solitary, presocial man, and sought to trace the movement from this "natural" condition to his current one as a social, political animal. Also like Hobbes, he thought that our principal concern was our self-preservation. He differed greatly, however, in his understanding of what is meant by "natural man."

Rather than a vanity-fueled, passionate aggressor, Rousseau's man possessed "two principles that are prior to reason"[6] one, already named, is self-preservation. The other, crucially, is "an innate repugnance to seeing his fellow men suffer" (p. 736), what we would call empathy.

Rousseau faulted Hobbes's account for speaking about "savage man, [when] it was civil man [he] depicted" (p. 725). That is, for Rousseau, vanity is a product of civilization. Therefore, if we

---

[5] Sonny Barger, Keith Zimmerman, and Kent Zimmerman, *Hell's Angel: The Life and Times of Sonny Barger and the Hell's Angels Motorcycle Club* (New York: Morrow, 2000), p. 124.

[6] Jean-Jacques Rousseau, *Discourse on the Origin and Foundations of Inequality Among Men*, in Morgan, *Classics*, p. 724.

change the type of political order we enter into we can change human nature. Hobbes's political order changed nothing about humans; it simply redirected the fear they had for each other to a fear of the government's power. For Rousseau (as he was to argue in another of his works, *The Social Contract*), if we change the type of political order, we can literally change human nature.

You may have heard Rousseau's human being referred to as a "noble savage," but he was neither. Rousseau's natural man was lacking in an ego, a sense of self. His natural man was "not evil precisely because [he does] not know what it is to be good" (p. 736). Wandering alone about in the forest, satisfying his hunger and thirst whenever they occurred, Rousseau's man had "neither foresight nor curiosity" (p. 731). Indeed, one might question whether Rousseau's natural man is a human at all: he lacks any capacity for self-reflection (owing to a lack of sense of self), and has no ability to recognize other selves as individuated human beings.

How do we account for the passage from this seemingly sub-human entity into a "civilized" person? For Rousseau, the simple facts of biology supplied the evolutionary impetus. Although men and women coupled at will, they didn't produce families because, owing to a lack of a sense of self, they were incapable of forming lasting relationships. However, owing to ongoing reproduction, the number of persons increased, and so did daily contact with others. This increasing contact slowly resulted in the acquisition of an ego and a sense of self: "this was the period of a first revolution which formed the establishment of the distinction among families and which introduced a kind of property" (p. 742).

For Rousseau, this was a halcyon time, at "an equal distance from the stupidity of brutes and the fatal enlightenment of civil man" (p. 743). This fleeting but measurable moment, "maintaining a middle position between the indolence of our primitive state and the petulant activity of our egocentrism, must have been the happiest and most durable epoch" (p. 743).

This middle period constitutes the ideal era of human existence, one that should be the goal of any future political order. "In proportion as ideas and sentiments succeed one another and as the mind and heart are trained, the human race continues to be tamed, relationships spread and bonds are tightened. People grew accustomed to gather in front of their huts or around a large tree; song and dance, true children of love and leisure, became the amusement or rather the occupation of idle men and women who flocked together" (p. 743). To live together in harmonious idleness, forming lasting emotional ties with one's brethren, whiling away the days singing and dancing—this was the ideal period of existence for humans.

Inevitably, however, "the first person who, having enclosed a plot of land, took it into his head to say this is mine and found people simple enough to believe him, was the true founder of civil society" (p. 740). Property became the external mirror of the ego, and out of this combination arose vanity, and "all the subsequent progress has been in appearance so many steps toward the perfection of the individual, and in fact toward the decay of the species" (p. 744). Civilization, far from improving humankind's condition, "for the profit of a few ambitious men henceforth subjected the entire human race to labor, servitude and misery" (p. 747). Rousseau argued a new political order must take us beyond degenerate "civilization," in a forward movement toward restoring a past condition, halfway between the brutes and the civilized. *The Social Contract* explains how we can bring about this transformation.

The motorcyclist has, in his own way, already managed a transition, however partial, out of civilization and into his own halcyon time by joining a motorcycle club. Hanging out at the state recreation area, building a bonfire, drinking with your brothers, working on your bike, the old ladies cooking and taking care of the kids, Steppenwolf blaring from speakers overhead—the motorcycle club enacts a scene from that golden Rousseauvian moment suspended between nature and civilization, the only difference being the presence of sleek internal combustion engines.

At a Labor Day club run, the motorcyclist has managed to regain the values of independence and brotherhood, values discarded by a middle class zealously seeking and protecting bourgeois comfort, willing to conform and isolate their striving families in suburbs and SUVs, fearful of others and protective of their property. The biker, through the motorcycle club, has regained a lost sense of community, a brotherhood that respects both independence and interdependence.

A True Nature's Child

While popular media have profited, literally, from sustaining the image of the Hobbesian, badass biker, we have seen that, from another perspective, the motorcyclist has chosen a way of life that corresponds to Rousseau's view of what is more authentically human. How do we treat this contradiction in the biker's image, simultaneously Hobbesian and Rousseauvian?

This primitive man, simultaneously a threat to society and its salvation, offers a useful conceptual framework for envisioning the motorcyclist, since contrasting our civilized values and behaviors with those of the primitive is a fundamentally ambiguous act. From the standpoint of bourgeois culture, the (Hobbesian) primitive could be a threat. But, from the point of view of the motorcycle club member, the Rousseauvian primitive could embody those positive human values lost to an alienated, consumerist society. Defining the primitive, however, is a vitally important social act, since defining the primitive simultaneously defines the civilized. The image of the motorcyclist as primitive allows us to show the ambiguous way he becomes socially manifest.

Here we approach the key to the puzzle of the motorcyclist as primitive. The concept of the "primitive" has emerged as a way to define what it means to be "civilized": while to the bourgeois, "primitive" may be a pejorative term, "civilized" and "primitive" merely reflect two opposing sets of social values. Fundamentally, the primitive and the civilized refer to implicit and conflicting notions of human nature, as well as human history. As "civilized" people, we believe social order can be established by proxy: we employ police, elect politicians, and conscript soldiers. A "primitive" understands that he must confront the world alone, or at least with a small band of like-minded brothers.

For the media, targeting middle-class consumers, the Hobbesian biker forms a negative yet titillating stereotype. Films such as *The Wild One* (1954) and *Hell's Angels on Wheels* (1967) allow viewers the fantasy experience of stepping over the boundary of acceptable behavior, to imaginatively participate in socially taboo acts. "They" terrorize towns, flaunt the legal system, use psychoactive drugs, engage in nonstandard sexual practices, and generally hold up a mirror to consumers to show them what they're not.

As J.M. Watson suggests, for the biker, "civilization," a place he finds "hostile, weak, and effeminate," is a useful negative pole from which to engage in the same activity as a civilized person, seeking an identity through opposition.[7] The club biker proudly identifies his separation from a so-called middle-class society that has branded his values as unacceptable. The middle class has lost the values of independence, brotherhood, and a willingness to stand up for itself. As a biker, I reject that softness; I am willing to stand up for myself and my values, even if that means doing so violently. As such, if I'm a biker, I must be doing something right. Both the nonrider and the biker are engaging in mutual acts of self-definition.

Both groups endorse Hobbesian individualism. The middle class sees the world economically as individually competitive, the spoils of which are embodied in consumerist "prizes": the suburban house, the SUV, the prestigious school for the kids. The biker is a badass: the world has to be confronted by an individual, unyielding will that establishes its supremacy.

Both groups endorse Rousseauvian community. The middle class, erecting walls, gates, and guards around its suburban enclave, protects its material possessions while simultaneously valuing others' right to theirs with neighborhood watch programs, entertainment events at the mall, and collective, competitive sports for the kids. The biker has the club run or the toy drive, where brothers can reaffirm their commitment to "freedom" and each other, and celebrate their success in living outside the constraints of a culture more concerned with getting and having than the joys of giving and simply being.

This reciprocal relationship highlights not an over- and underclass, or the moral and the depraved, or the progressive and the backward, but a conflict in values. The suburban bourgeois, leaving her suburban community burbclave, racing toward the mall in her aggressively styled, screw-the-environment gas guzzler while shouting into her cell phone, openly

---

[7] J.M. Watson, "Outlaw Motorcyclists: An Outgrowth of Lower-Class Cultural Concerns," *Deviant Behavior: An Interdisciplinary Journal* 2 (1980), pp. 31–48.

displays signs of her vanity-feeding affluence, demonstrating visually her superiority to those around her. The leather-clad biker, the primitive steering himself through life on ape-hangers alongside his club members is, through his rejection of straight society, engaging in a positive, life-affirming act: there is freedom in the wind. The motorcyclist rejects the idea of human nature underlying straight society, and endorses a romantic return to the values of individualism and freedom that are achieved on the open road, hauling ass down the highway.

LAST LEG:
400 Miles

Life and pleasure appear to be inseparable, for pleasure never arises without activity, and, equally, it completes every activity.

—ARISTOTLE (*Nicomachean Ethics*, Book X, Chapter 4, 19–21)

12

Leather-Clad: Eroticism, Fetishism, and other -isms in Biker Fashion

SUZANNE FERRISS

Q: Why do motorcycle gangs wear leather?
A: Because chiffon wrinkles so easily.

This old joke actually raises some interesting issues about motorcycle fashion. Bikers don't generally wear chiffon, not because it wrinkles necessarily, but because it wouldn't offer any protection against the elements. Leather can keep the rider warm, protected from wind, rain, and (sometimes) pavement. Consider laying a bike down wearing chiffon! But the joke is not really making an argument about utility. It's about the image of the biker. Motorcycle "gangs" wouldn't be caught dead in chiffon. Chiffon is for girls and wimps. Motorcyclists are simply too tough and their fabric of choice—leather—embodies their power.

Utilitarian arguments—about the usefulness of a particular fabric or garment—can in no way account for biker fashion, or fashion in general. Fashion is not simply about clothes, but clothes in relation to the body and to our culture. In a sense, fashion is a visible language that carries meanings that change over time and within cultures. Fashion means clothing that *changes*.[1] Why and how it changes in contemporary culture is intertwined with our notions of sexuality and gender. Biker fashion, specifically leather and its connections with eroticism, fetishism, and other -isms, reflects shifting ideas about men, women, and motorcycling.

---

[1] For a good overview of the development and possible approaches to modern fashion see Elizabeth Wilson, *Adorned in Dreams: Fashion and Modernity* (Berkeley: University of California Press, 1987).

Motorcycles, Leather, and Sex

Fashion is inevitably associated with sexuality, owing to its intimate connection to the body. Clothing plays a role in sexual attraction because it both reveals and conceals the body. It also contributes to our sense of gender—whether a particular member of one sex (male or female) appears masculine or feminine, either enhancing or detracting from their attractiveness to us as potential partners. Motorcycle fashion complicates these associations, for, as fashion historian Valerie Steele has noted, "the mystique of the motorcycle is . . . strongly associated with leather and sex."[2]

Sometimes we sexualize the motorcycle itself. We call sport bikes "crotch rockets" for a reason. A rider mounts his bike and embarks on a journey that excites the senses. Fused with the machine, the rider experiences intense exhilaration and release. While this image privileges male sexuality, female riders are often quizzed whether their enjoyment comes in part from the vibration of the machine between their legs. But few riders— male or female—would answer that the feel of the machine alone makes the motorcycle sexy. Instead, the sexual allure of motorcycling comes from a set of more complicated associations of motorcycling with risk and rebellion played out on the body through clothing.

For instance, a male biker's leather jacket associates him with images of toughness and masculinity. It makes him "cool," because we connect him to the iconic, leather-clad bikers popularized in films of the 1950s such as James Dean in *Rebel Without a Cause* (1955) and Marlon Brando in *The Wild One* (1954). The famous promotional still from the *The Wild One* displays Brando slouched confidently against a black 600 cc Triumph Speed Twin. He wears leather gloves, jeans rolled up over boots, and a military cap tilted at a rakish, devil-may-care angle. With his leather jacket zipped almost to the top, he exposes just a hint of neck.[3]

---

[2] Valerie Steele, *Fetish: Fashion, Sex, and Power* (New York: Oxford University Press, 1996), p. 154.

[3] Ironically, some male bikers who saw *The Wild One* did not identify with the leather-clad Johnny (Brando), but with his film buddy Chino (Lee Marvin), who wore a black and yellow striped shirt. The head of the Los Angeles Hells Angels actually left the film to buy his "bumblebee" shirt.

Women unsettle this equation of leather with masculinity. Think Bike Week in Daytona Beach, Florida, with its parade of bikini-clad women wearing only leather chaps for coverage They expose their sexuality, but not simply by exposing flesh. Instead, they take advantage of the contrast between the softness of their bare flesh and the toughness of the leather that partially conceals it. The interplay between leather and flesh adds to their allure.

This same contrast works when women wear full leather, especially if there is some suggestion of the flesh beneath. A tight leather suit, for instance, highlights the curves of the female body. A zipper open to reveal cleavage invites speculation about what else is hidden. The British film *Girl on a Motorcycle* (1968), starring Marianne Faithfull, exploits this contrast, featuring a frustrated newlywed riding a huge black Harley through Germany to visit her lover. In the film (and in the novel on which it is based), the motorcycle itself is presented as a sexual object.[4] It is her "black bull." She rides wearing her leather riding suit, but her real sexual pleasure comes from the knowledge that she is naked under her suit. (The X-rated version was called *Naked Under Leather* in America.) The sexual fantasies she entertains as she rides all focus on her lover peeling away the leather to reveal the flesh beneath.

Leather's association with masculine toughness shapes not only heterosexual but homosexual desire. Policemen and cowboys, in addition to motorcyclists, are important gay male icons. Leather boys and leather men embody a virile male sexuality attractive to some gay men for its equation with power. For both heterosexuals and homosexuals, leather signals masculine toughness. For this reason, leather features prominently in sado-masochistic (S&M) rituals in props—whips, dog collars, belts—to establish dominance. Motorcycling, homosexuality, and S&M come together not simply in the porno section of your local video store but in Kenneth Anger's cult classic film *Scorpio Rising* (1964) which features an army of gay Nazi bikers.

Masculinity, Power, and Fetishism

The biker's black leather jacket became associated with toughness partly for historical reasons. Motorcycle clubs such as the

---

[4] André Pieyre de Mandiargues, *The Motorcycle* (*La Motocyclette*, 1963).

one featured in *The Wild One* originated with the returning GIs after WWII. Seeking camaraderie and adventure in a world of "civilians," they organized the Boozefighters and other motorcycle clubs. Their shared association with a military past extended even to their clothing, borrowed from their military uniform. The black leather jacket originated with German aviators of WWI, such as the famous Red Baron. Later associations with the Nazis further equated leather with power and domination. Early riders adapted the protective leather armor of wartime battle for the road, retaining their military garb for both protection and solidarity with their riding buddies. Even early female riders, such as Theresa Wallach, who in 1935 was the first person of either sex to make the north-south crossing of the African continent (7,500 miles) on two wheels, chose to wear desert fatigues and goggles. Nearly two decades earlier, when sisters Augusta and Adeline Van Buren rode cross-country on individual motorcycles in 1916 to prove to the military that women were able to ride as dispatch couriers for the war effort, they were arrested numerous times en route for wearing men's clothes.

At this point, you may be thinking: Biker history is all well and good, but what does it have to do with philosophy? A lot, it turns out, because leather and power have everything to do with a key concept in twentieth-century Western political philosophy and philosophy of mind: the fetish object. The contemporary biker, whose leather jacket does not share this past, still benefits from the association of leather and power, though in a much more complicated way. The black leather jacket has become a fetish object.

A fetish is an object that we make and endow with magical properties. The magical properties of the fetish protect us against our fears. There are two forms of fetishism: psychosexual and commodity fetishism. The biker's leathers are caught up in both definitions.

Psychologically, fetishism manages gender anxieties about whether one is sufficiently masculine or feminine. According to psychoanalyst Sigmund Freud, the fetish object wards off fears of castration in men. Afraid that their sexual potency will be diminished in contact with an actual partner, men turn a benign part of the female body or an object associated with it into a nonthreatening substitute. Owing to its connection to the body, clothing is particularly likely to be fetishized. To cite an extreme example, some men can become sexually aroused by high heels—not on women but as objects in their own right. The shoe can serve as a tangible reminder of an absent female wearer or substitute for the body itself, leading to sexual arousal in the male who sees, sniffs, or holds it. One man, for instance, kissed one rose-colored slipper while ejaculating into the other (Steele, *Fetish*, p. 98).

While the shoe diminishes female sexual power for men, the black leather jacket augments male potency. In Freudian terms, it becomes a token of masculine power against any potential feminine threat. By putting on the black leather jacket, a man acquires the toughness and virility associated with it. Your average male Harley rider—no Boozefighter or Hells Angel (but more likely your dentist or accountant)—can feel masculine, sexually attractive, and powerful simply by donning his jacket.

Freudian explanations are more complicated for women. (Freud famously asked, "What do women want?" and then couldn't answer in his essay "On Femininity.") Since women are, in effect, already castrated, according to Freud, they have nothing to fear. But you could argue that they might like to feel more powerful and could do so by putting on the same jacket invested with the magical properties of toughness.[5] A woman could become like a dominatrix, finding pleasure in having power over men.

However, if she fears being identified as "masculine" or as one of the proud "dykes on bikes," she may instead wear the jacket ironically to highlight the contrast between the masculine hardness of leather and her feminine softness. Think, for instance, of the lady bikers who wear pink leather or jackets "bedazzled" with rhinestones. They are trying to be tough, to be taken seriously as bikers, but not so tough that they can't be imagined as wives, mothers, or grandmothers. Dot Robinson, the first president of the first women's motorcycle club, The

---

[5] For feminist readings, see essays by Emily Apter, Jann Matlock, Naomi Schor, and Elizabeth Grosz, in Emily Apter and William Pietz, ed., *Fetishism as Cultural Discourse* (Ithaca: Cornell University Press, 1993). Also see Lorraine Gamman and Merja Makinen, *Female Fetishism* (New York: NYU Press, 1994, 1995); Kaja Silverman, *Male Subjectivity at the Margins* (New York: Routledge, 1992); and Laura Mulvey, *Fetishism and Curiosity* (Bloomington: Indiana University Press, 1996).

Motor Maids, founded in the 1940s, insisted on wearing pink and even attached a lipstick holder to her Harley to make "people realize that not all of us are like the bearded, black-leather-jacketed hoods that the media tars us with."[6] The contemporary members of the club tell their "favorite story" about Dot on their website. It's from a Honda dealer in Sarasota, Florida who "chased that woman for two days, through mud and trees" but never caught her. At the end of the race, while the men hit the local bar, Dot returned to her room to clean up, eventually appearing in the bar "in a black sheath dress and a pill box hat." The lesson for the Motor Maids? "Dot was always a lady."[7]

Consumerism and Commodity Fetishism

Another way of thinking about the black leather jacket as a fetish object links it to consumerism. According to German philosopher Karl Marx (1818–1883), all commodities are fetishes. The things we buy exist in our minds apart from the human labor that constructed them. We mistakenly value the thing, independently of the human work that created it. Things appear in the stores as if by magic and become entities endowed with special properties.

Marx distinguishes in his book *Capital* between a commodity's "use value" and its "exchange value." "Use value" refers to the fact that, as an external object, as a thing, a product satisfies certain needs. A leather jacket keeps you warm and protects you from the elements. A product only becomes a commodity when it is "transferred to [another] person, for whom it serves as a use value, through the medium of exchange."[8] Its "exchange value" refers to what the object can be exchanged for in the market, that is, what you'd be willing to pay for the jacket. This value is independent of its utility and instead is shaped by its value within the economy.

---

[6] Quoted in Ann Ferrar, *Hear Me Roar: Women, Motorcycle and the Rapture of the Road*, second edition (North Conway:Whitehorse Press, 2001), p. 29.

[7] *Motor Maids, Inc.*, "Dot Robinson, Co-Founder of the Motor Maids," http://www.motormaids.org/dotlady.html

[8] Karl Marx, *Capital: A Critique of Political Economy*, Volume 1 (London: Penguin, 1976), p. 131. Subsequent page references are included in the text.

The jacket is not simply pieces of leather that someone has stitched together. If it were, the only difference among jackets might be the quality of the leather, the degree of artistry visible in its construction, or the amount of time the seamstress labored to produce it. Instead, in our minds we endow some jackets with additional value that cannot be easily measured in terms of the amount of fabric or the hours of labor. Some of us, for instance, are willing to pay more for a jacket with the Harley-Davidson insignia than one without.

Marx argues that "a commodity appears at first sight an extremely obvious, trivial thing. But its analysis brings out that it is a very strange thing, abounding in metaphysical subtleties and theological niceties" (p. 163). He offers the example of a wooden table. By his labor, a man shapes a material from nature, wood, into a useful object. But "the table continues to be wood, an ordinary, sensuous thing" (p. 163). However, once we buy it and put it in our living room, "it changes into a thing which transcends sensuousness. It not only stands with its feet on the ground, but in relation to all other commodities, it stands on its head, and evolves out of its wooden brain grotesque ideas, far more wonderful than if it were to begin dancing of its own free will" (pp. 163–64). It's hard reading this not to envision some Disney-esque animated table dancing around the living room! But the table's magical properties are not the fantasy of an animator but a product of our own minds. The table has an independent existence in our brains, colored by its associations to other objects, such as the couch and chairs that surround it, and separate from the natural material and the human labor that produced it. It becomes, for instance, just the thing to bring the whole room together!

Marx offers the analogy of religion: "There the products of the human brain appear as autonomous figures endowed with a life of their own, which enter into relations both with each other and with the human race" (p. 165). Like the gods that peopled the brains of the Greeks, commodities acquire a power that we invest in them apart from their usefulness or the skill or artistry of their producer.

Branded with the Harley-Davidson insignia, for example, the biker's jacket becomes not only a symbol of masculine power but acquires the particular qualities consumers associate with the company, such as Americanness and rugged individualism.

The distinctive orange-and-black color scheme announces that this is not a motorcycle jacket but a Harley product. It's not a simple protective garment but a fetish object, calling to mind images of tough leather-clad riders cruising the roads on their Harleys.

The case of the nonrider is even more interesting. Anyone can walk into a motorcycle store and buy the products associated with riding simply to *look as if* they ride. Completely divorced from the actual rider or the motorcycle, the jacket branded with the H-D logo stands in for motorcycling itself. The jacket then becomes a magical object, capable of transferring to its wearer the properties of aggression, independence, and anti-authoritarianism, to name just a few. Simply by purchasing products, ordinary middle-class consumers can pose as rebels without taking the actual risks of riding.

Marketers cash in on motorcycling culture by selling the mystique—even to those who cannot ride. Young consumers-in-training can buy their Harley Ken or Bratz Boy Cade, each sporting his own miniature jacket. (Apparently, the biker chick passenger shown on the box is not included.) Motorcycling itself is marketed to children as a masculine pursuit, which, even though the boys themselves could probably not care less at this age, will eventually get them girls.

At its extreme as a commodity fetish, biker gear becomes fashion totally removed from motorcycling. In the early 1990s, a spread in *Vogue* called "Biker Chic" featured a gaggle of supermodels wearing short skirts, clunky motorcycle boots, leather jackets and Brando-esque caps. In the image, they stand close together, blocking two motorcycles posed behind them, their wheels visible only at the edges of the frame. The motorcycles are completely beside the point, which is the sale of leather clothing designed by Claude Montana, Calvin Klein, and others. No wonder that, in 1991, the Council of Fashion Designers of America recognized Harley-Davidson for its influence on fashion.

The motorcycle jacket has become so common in fashion design, in fact, that in 2004 it earned its own exhibit at the Phoenix Art Museum. The exhibit surveyed how fashion designers, such as Karl Lagerfeld, Roberto Cavalli, Moschino, and Dolce & Gabbana, have interpreted the "look of the motorcycle jacket in their creations." While jackets themselves were on display—including one custom tailored for Elvis Presley—the focus was more on the "look," on how the jacket has been reconfigured by designers. Another highlight of the exhibit was a Bob Mackie ensemble worn by Cher in Las Vegas in the 1980s, Swarovski crystals and all. In the words of the exhibit's promoters, "Here, biker style is off-road and center stage."[9] Off-road, indeed.

The Motorcycle as Fashion Accessory

At the extreme of fetishism, motorcycles themselves become merely fashion accessories, props in ads to sell Skechers sneakers or Soft&Dri deodorant. The bike featured now is not typically the cruiser associated with the dominant image of the motorcyclist emerging in the 1950s. Instead, it is the sport bike, the "crotch rocket" chosen for speed and associated with an altered image of the biker.

As commodities, motorcycles themselves are subject to changes in design. They are aesthetic objects equally subject to the vicissitudes of fashion. To many young riders, the cruiser is now inseparable from its forty-plus-something demographic—it's old. Instead, the sleek design of the sport bike captures the pace of youth. *Biker Boyz* and *Torque* have supplanted the *Wild One* in the popular imagination of at least younger riders.

Leather—now colored, not black—links the rider to the bike. It's common practice to select riding gear to match the motorcycle—even the helmet, which, it could be argued, is worn more for style than protection. As a result, the rider merges with the machine in a blur of color from head to wheel. In full racing leathers, the rider appears androgynous—neither male nor female—nor even a person but an extension of the machine itself.

Uncoupled from its associations with a tough and rebellious male rider, the sport bike appears to stand for speed and youth. It's the new fashion in motorcycling. Advertisers are cashing in on its sexiness in a different sense—as new and popular, not necessarily erotic. (After all, deodorant is hardly sexy.)

---

[9] Phoenix Art Museum website, Past Exhibitions, "Motorcycle Jacket," www.phxart.org/pastexhibitions/motorcyclejacket.asp.

13

The Wild One, She-Devils on Wheels, and "Motorcycle Syndrome": Foucault and Biker Images

GARY L. KIEFFNER

When riding a Harley out on an isolated, open road for several hours, it's easy to start imagining yourself differently. You have finally escaped from all of the subtle mud and oppression of everyday life, to experience selfhood and solitude in nature. There are no telephones. No crowds, no barking dogs or other obnoxious noises. Just you with your powerful engine, the Road, and the sound and feel of the wind. As you become one with the machine, you may feel like a centaur, a roaming creature of the forest. Or a siren, as your pipes play your compelling, alluring music. Or Robin Hood on an ancient proletarian mission. Or you may see yourself as debonair Pancho Villa, empowered Cher, Billy Idol or Britney Spears, or Jesse James on the ultimate chopper.

Yet, no matter how twentieth- and twenty-first-century riders have imagined themselves while operating their motorcycles, these self-identities and fantasies have been socially ignored and reworked by a variety of nonriders, institutions, and social power structures. The result has been a stifling, negative set of stereotypes and attempts to alienate motorcyclists.

You probably have an idea what I'm talking about here. We'll get into some interesting examples later. Bikers, in turn, individually and collectively responded to these negative stereotypes. While such processes have taken many forms over the years, in this chapter we'll focus on how the world of motorcycling has become sexually charged largely because of how larger societal explanations, studies, and descriptions of biker sexuality have exerted their influence. This sexualization of bikers by larger sociopolitical forces has occurred for many decades and continues up to the present day.

The shifting relationships among actual motorcyclists, imagined bikers, and nonriders are very revealing. The ideas of the French philosopher Michel Foucault (1926–1984) will help us look at how particular public images of motorcyclists slowly developed, how they became sexual stereotypes, and a few ways in which these myths interacted with real bikers and non-riders.[1] We will see that there are forces out there that are larger than motorcycling, and that these forces seek to control and eventually dominate riders. These forces work their mojo partially through specific sexual explanations and images of bikers.

Foucault's terminology, or anything having to do with his theories, is called "Foucauldian." Thus, Foucault's theories applied to social dynamics is known as "Foucauldian discourse." "Power center" means the causes, effects, and workings of an institution as well as the institution itself. A power center could be governmental, private, corporate, or special interest–oriented—for example, the American Medical Association. A Foucauldian "power structure" consists of two or more power centers working with each other or in opposition to each other, within the same system—such as the American Medical Association working toward its goals that coincide with those of both the Food and Drug Administration and social rules and values, resulting in uniformity of norms and conformity. American capitalist society is another example of a power structure, and a big, complicated one at that.

Deploying Sexuality—Who Does It to Whom

The "deployment of sexuality," one of Foucault's key terms, refers to the ways in which power centers cause sexuality to be talked about, published, displayed, thought about, or imagined. An example of a deployment of biker sexuality would be the California Attorney General's 1965 official report stating that bik-ers commit "sex perversion" and a subsequent *Newsweek* article, which mistakenly reports that the Attorney General "accused"

---

[1] Unless otherwise noted, page numbers in parentheses will refer to Michel Foucault, *The History of Sexuality, Volume 1: An Introduction* (New York: Random House, 1990).

the male bikers in question of being gay.[2] Such governmental and media-generated deployments of sexuality convey information or dis-information concerning sex and bikers for specific purposes.

Some examples of Foucauldian power centers include the medical profession, the movie industry, the print media, the Harley-Davidson Motor Company, and police agencies. These all try to exert various kinds of control over, among others, motorcyclists, people who consider their self-identities in terms of lesbian, gay, bisexual, transsexual, or transgendered (LGBT), or those who regard themselves as members of both categories (namely, LGBT riders).

"Motorcycle Syndrome"—A Medical Deployment of Sexuality

Foucault considers the psychiatric and psychological professions' role as a power center. Applying this to motorcycling, a prime example of Foucauldian biker sexuality discourse would include an article published in *Time* magazine on December 7th, 1970, titled "The Motorcycle Syndrome." Reading the article with Foucault in mind, the psychiatric profession and the weekly news press attempted to medicalize the desire to ride motorcycles as a mental illness. According to the anonymous *Time* author, who describes the work of a Harvard Medical School psychiatrist, enthusiasm for motorcycle riding is "a hitherto unrecognized emotional ailment" and the psychiatrist "found the same basic symptoms in all his sick cyclists." Such supposed symptoms included promiscuity, impotency, and being "always worried about discovering that they were homosexuals." The article claims that riders "used their motorcycles to compensate for feelings of effeminacy and weakness" (p. 65).

One may think that mainstream medical professionals couldn't possibly take such ideas seriously, but they actually did. In fact, this doctor's theories about motorcyclists were published in the *American Journal of Psychiatry* and he was also cited in *Dun's*

---

[2] "Accused" is the term used by Hunter S. Thompson in his own published contribution to this deployment of sexuality. See Thompson, "The Motorcycle Gangs: Losers and Outsiders," *Nation* 200, No. 20 (May 17th, 1965), pp. 522–26, especially p. 523.

Review (January 1972, p. 44). Such acceptance and dissemination of his research represents a significant deployment of sexuality by one power center, the psychiatric profession—as part of a larger power structure, the medical profession in collusion with the press—against motorcyclists. The results for the power structure at hand—the medical profession—included individual and collective prestige and power enhancement, increased subjugation, and control. By identifying and exploiting motorcyclists, the power structure gained knowledge and profit for itself, while at the same time it marginalized riders as a group.

Control of Sex Objects—Media, Gender, Jails, and Capitalism

Sexuality deployments take other forms as well, including the objectification of women who ride motorcycles. We can find a colorful example back in 1916, when Adeline and Augusta Van Buren rode across North America to prove that women are capable of serving as U.S. army dispatch riders. (Swift messenger service was an important military concern in the days before the development of radio technology.) The Van Buren sisters dressed the part: they wore military-style leggings and their riding breeches were made of leather. However, the Foucauldian discourse generated by their visit to Denver, Colorado, is mean-spirited. The *Denver Post* printed a degrading article about the riders that read, "The [national] preparedness issue was serving as an excellent excuse for women to stay away from home, to display physical prowess in various fields of masculine superiority, and to display their feminine contours in nifty khaki and leather uniforms."[3]

Due to nonmotorcyclist reactions to these "feminine contours," several times out in the middle of America, in small towns between Ohio and the Rocky Mountains, "the Man" incarcerated the Van Buren sisters. They were accused of bogus infractions such as "wearing men's clothing." But each time they

---

[3] Anne Tully Ruderman, "The Daring Escapade of 1916," *Ms.* 6–8 (February 1978), pp. 54–55; Anne "Tulle" Ruderman and Jo Giovannoni, "Adeline and Augusta Van Buren . . . Pioneers in Women in Motorcycling," *Asphalt Angels* 74 (September–October, 1998), pp. 11–15.

were arrested, the cops—after detaining them for a while—released them, advising them to leave town immediately.

One wonders whether the women's corporate sponsorships—by Firestone Tires and Indian Moto-Cycles—had anything to do with their relatively quick releases and immediate expulsions. Hmmmmm. Could this be a case of Foucauldian collusion between two power centers—the town leadership and the transportation industry—within one power structure?

First, there were arrests in order to restrain and control women within established gender roles. This served as a warning to local town women not to try what those two city women are doing. Then, a quick release of the sisters under the condition that they leave immediately. This ensured that few other women in town would see them. Also, the quicker they got to California, the sooner Indian and Firestone could sell more products. This is a classic example of how Foucauldian discourse and a deployment of sexuality operate. (See? It's really quite simple. We've all witnessed deployments of sexuality, though maybe not as dramatic as this one.)

The *Denver Post* article certainly betrays the author's sexual objectification of women, if nothing else. By the 1920s, photographers were already selling pictures of women posing provocatively, mounted on bikes in a style that would later become typical of an *Easyriders* centerfold. This emerging exploitation of an imagined biker sexuality was gradually increased and intensified in the second half of the century by the power structure known as the media, following the Foucauldian model. According to Foucault, "The deployment of sexuality has its reason for being in proliferating, innovating, annexing, creating, and penetrating bodies in an increasingly detailed way, and in controlling populations in an increasingly comprehensive way" (p. 107).

So, it shouldn't be surprising that, by the end of the century, Teah Chadderdon of Northern Arizona University statistically demonstrated extensive sexploitation of women in motorcycle magazines. After compiling statistics using 2,653 images of females in twenty-two recent publications, she found that 46.1 percent of the subjects were either nude, wearing swimming suits, or barely dressed.[4]

---

[4] Teah Chadderdon, "Marketing Gender: Bodies or Bikes?" A paper delivered

Pictorial images of scantily-clad women are indeed problematic, although it is worth mentioning another aspect beyond Chadderdon's field of analysis: the fact that this represents exploitation of "motorcyclists"—in this case women who are *supposedly* motorcyclists—*by the media*, a Foucauldian power structure. Because 1970s and 1980s magazines such as *Easyriders*, *Iron Horse*, and *Biker*, which supposedly depicted the post-hippie motorcycle lifestyle, sold far more copies than the small population of hardcore bikers could have purchased, it becomes obvious that the readership of these biker rags must have been predominantly nonbiker. Pictures of so-called biker chicks were popular among nonriders from the 1960s through the end of the millennium. Late in the century, mainstream advertising campaigns capitalized on such sexual discourse by featuring female "bikers" in conjunction with themes like sado-masochism, bondage and domination, and lesbianism. The press promoted an objectification and erotic imagining of women motorcyclists, by riding and nonriding men, through the deployment of biker sexual stereotypes.

Sex in the Machine—Literary and Corporate Deployments

Another print media–based deployment of sexuality stems from certain literary descriptions of how the ride feels. Harley-Davidson typically utilized an antiquated, dual-fire ignition system with a 45-degree V-twin configuration for most of the century, until 1998. It vibrated. In fact, it vibrated *very nicely*. Some authors describe the sensation of riding in language that was overtly sensual or sexual.[5]

But how intensely a small percentage of Harley enthusiasts may have enjoyed its unique vibration is irrelevant. What is important in a discussion of Foucauldian discourse is that such

---

at the Southwest / Texas Popular Culture Association Annual Conference, Albuquerque, New Mexico (March 9th, 2001), p. 33.

[5] Gail DeMarco, *Rebels with a Cause: We Ride the Harley* (Santa Rosa: Squarebooks, 1994), p. 120; Brock Yates, *Outlaw Machine: Harley-Davidson and the Search for the American Soul* (New York: Little, Brown, 1999), p. 133. Trisha Yeager, *How to Be Sexy With Bugs in Your Teeth* (Chicago: Contemporary Books, 1978), pp. 2–3.

authors either sensationalized a largely unknown phenomenon, or they confessed a description of their own sensuality, or they interviewed women to solicit confession of their sensual and sexual experiences. These personal moments were published, distributed, studied, and relished.

This dynamic matches the Foucauldian deployment model as the authors disseminate information, perpetuate a myth or mystique, and set up motorcyclists as sexual objects to be exploited and controlled. "Mystique" is a word that Harley-Davidson Motor Company uses to refer to its version of this and other imaginary constructions of riders and the ride. A 1993 video, produced by the Motor Company to narrate the history of the company and its bikes, deploys this concept repeatedly. Actor James Caan mentions the mystique as he *slowwwwly* mounts a late model Harley and refers to visual features of the V-shaped engine and sensual elements—"how great it feels to ride."[6] Caan uses the word "erotic" and connects the Harley Mystique to the product itself and what it might do to make people happy. (Since the Harley-Davidson Motor Company made the film in order to make people want to buy Harley-Davidson motorcycles and related products, naturally Harleys are portrayed as having attractive qualities.)

But there is something else to consider. Cultural philosophy and history are partly influenced by commercial films like this one, so they too must be examined as tools for deploying sexuality, to tighten the control over riders (and their spending habits) and, thus, increase the company's power (while maximizing the accumulation of wealth). The Harley video is important because it mentions sexual elements, shows that they started early on, and portrays them as something desirable. It actually deploys sexuality to increase company control of a target market and population through sales, followed by automatic membership in HOG—the Harley Owners Group, another power center. Since the purpose of the film footage is to increase the power-knowledge-pleasure of a Foucauldian power structure, the video must be taken seriously.

---

[6] Joel T. Smith, director, *Harley-Davidson: The American Motorcycle*, featuring James Caan, David Crosby, and Wynonna Judd (Cabin Fever, 1993), videocassette.

Increasingly Restrictive Definitions—What Is a Biker?

Thus, capitalist power centers such as Harley-Davidson Motor Company, HOG, the media, the psychiatric profession, segments of nonriding society, and motorcyclists interacted with each other, leading to the development and redevelopment of customs, norms, rules, and stereotypes. Considering the popular, nonriding societal myth about bikers that slowly changed from the 1950s through the rest of the century, their biker sexual images may be considered as increasingly defined social constructions for the purpose of alienation, marginalization, and domination. The power structures attempted to control bikers by placing them at a social distance away from everyone else, via the tactic of developing *the* definition of "biker" more precisely.

By the 1980s the main biker male stereotype became that of the "scooter tramp." Examples of scooter tramp archetypical figures include Captain America and Billy in the film *Easy Rider* (1969), the 1970s underground comic character Easy Wolf, Gar in Peter Bogdanovich's *Mask* (1985), Harley from *Harley-Davidson and the Marlboro Man* (1991), and the earlier legendary versions of Sonny Barger and of Spider from *Easyriders* magazine. Because he is imagined as a "tramp," this automatically creates a social distance separating "scooter" people from everyone else. Once separated, a group may be more easily controlled.

Of course, not all bikers were male. Anthropologist Barbara Joans describes two other mythic gender constructs that emerged during this era in her 1997 essay "Women Who Ride: The Bitch in the Back is Dead." According to Joans, if the woman rode on the back, she was stereotyped by the public as a "sexual outlaw": sexually promiscuous, insatiable, and possibly bisexual. If she operated her own bike, she was also labeled a "gender traitor" who transgressed gender norms by taking control of a "masculine" machine. The "gender traitor's" imagined ambiguous sexuality made her scary to nonriders.[7] Thus, female motorcycle operators were relegated to the margins of society.

---

[7] Barbara Joans, "Women Who Ride: The Bitch in the Back is Dead," in Anne Bolin and Jane Granskog, eds., *Athletic Intruders: Ethnographic Research on Women, Culture, and Exercise* (Albany: State University of New York Press, 2003 [1997]).

The public display of a woman's body, clothed but fully visible at eye level, on a motorcycle—whether on the back or the front seat but especially as operator—was a symbol of excessive mobility, especially after the end of World War II when gender roles were redefined and car seat heights were lowered. According to this anti-gay, misogynous world view, a woman on a motorcycle had placed a phallus between her legs and had no legitimate business on that bike.

Movies and the Deployment of Biker "Chicks"

One Foucauldian power center, the movie industry, further developed motorcyclist images and perpetuated a more clearly-defined, stereotypical "biker chick" from the 1960s through the 1970s even while actual riders adopted elements of her attitude, her fictional imagined lifestyle, and her costume as their wardrobe. Stereotypical sexual elements of this creature were portrayed in film. For example, in *Teenage Gang Debs* (1966), female characters create sexual chaos in a love triangle, convince one man to kill another, and enact lesbian sexuality in front of god and everybody. The female rider is depicted as a crazed, dangerous bisexual.

Other movies such as Jack Cardiff's *Girl on a Motorcycle*, released in 1968, catered to straight male–centered fantasies such as sadomasochism, predation, and unbridled sexuality. The entire movie consists of actress Marianne Faithfull's character Rebecca leaving her nonriding husband and traveling on her Harley to meet her lover. She stops and gets drunk at a roadhouse, then continues onward. She rides along on her saddle, intoxicated, and starts to become aroused. As her body writhes and moves, she addresses the bike. "My black devil, you make love beautifully . . . Take me to him, my black pimp!"[8] (Although the motorcycle's paint was solid gloss black, the dual entendre also refers to the "African-American, street-level, sex broker" racial stereotype.) She becomes so aroused that she nearly crashes. Dozens of biker flicks sexualized the female biker image as an irresponsible, brainless nymphomaniac.

---

[8] Jack Cardiff, director, *Girl on a Motorcycle*, featuring Marianne Faithful, Alain Delon, and Roger Mutton (Warner Brothers, 1968), videocassette.

Even so, at least one of these productions might be described as empowering during the 1960s, a time of gendered inequality and resistance. The 1968 Hershell Gordon Lewis movie *She-Devils on Wheels* is a landmark biker film in terms of the fictive portrayal of gender role *inversion*. The all-female gang members regularly race each other to find out who gets first choice of the passive, hang-around males for the night.[9] This movie was so different from the other forty-some odd biker movies released between 1966 and 1972, especially in its inversion of genders, that *She-Devils* alone has recently been selected to be reproduced and will probably come out soon, with the same title. (Pun *intended*. But I may be wrong about that; we'll have to wait and see the movie to find out. . . .)

Virtually all of the biker films made during this era included sexual content that made them integral to a Foucauldian deployment of sexuality.

Targeting Motorcyclists for Elimination

Such portrayed images, along with other types of Foucauldian discourse, historically led to legal restrictions. According to Foucault:

> The law would be secure, even in the new mechanics of power. For this is the paradox of a society which . . . has created so many technologies of power that are foreign to the concept of law: it fears the effects and proliferation of those technologies and attempts to recode them in forms of law. (p. 109)

Joans discusses socio-legal, nonrider backlash against motorcyclists and explains that because the predominant masculine biker image was one of danger, courage, and a lifestyle of liberty, the public targets them for elimination.[10] Put in Foucauldian terms, the legal and legislative power centers fear biker sexuality and crack down on motorcyclists as an entire community.

---

[9] Hershell Gordon Lewis, director, *She-Devils on Wheels*, featuring Betty Connell, Nancy Lee Noble, and Christie Wagner (Mayflower Pictures/Western World Video, 1968), videocassette.

Deployment of the Gay Biker and Its Effects

Queer male biker imagery—along with much of the power-structural fear of motorcyclists—can historically be traced to *The Wild One*, a 1954 László Benedek film classic. When the movie was released, some straight males complained about Marlon Brando's biker character Johnny; his leather costume, cap, and body language were considered too effeminate. Viewers called Johnny a "fag" and instead rooted for Lee Marvin's character Chico, who was considered to resemble a real biker. Nonriders feared both gays and bikers, while some riders also used homophobic language.

Yet, the image of Brando as Johnny became a fetish in gay male culture for the rest of the century and, in the long run, also became a dominant straight biker image. Thus, *The Wild One* was a queering of motorcycle imagery and culture by Hollywood, a major media power structure, since the antihero did not dress like or act like the typical motorcyclists of the period but, instead, influenced later motorcycle fashions and iconography as well as queer pleasure.

In the Mexican American Borderlands, however, Brando's machismo was considered realistic. As Eric Zolov writes in *Refried Elvis: The Rise of the Mexican Counterculture*, Brando, James Dean, and Elvis Presley were thought of as *rebeldes sin causa*, "rebels without a cause." But it was Presley who fell from graceland (Sorry about that; it was too tempting. I promise not to insert any more silly puns), after the media in Mexico reported a remark that he allegedly made in an interview—something to the effect that he would rather kiss three African American women than "a Mexican."

The report (which later turned out to be false) was a smear tactic enacted by a traditional, older generational power center trying to turn younger people away from rock 'n' roll. Nonetheless, the immediate public reaction against Presley centered not on race but on his sexual preferences. Young people in Mexico and the borderlands dismissed him as gay. As an

---

[10] Barbara Joans, "Dykes on Bikes Meet Ladies of Harley," in William L. Leap, ed., *Beyond the Lavender Lexicon: Authenticity, Imagination, and Appropriation in Lesbian and Gay Languages* (Luxembourg: Gordon and Breach, 1995), pp. 87–106.

imagined *joto*, he was thereafter permanently considered effeminate in a culture that valued machismo.[11]

Presley and James Dean were bikers, while Brando played the role of a motorcyclist in the movies and is more widely imagined as a biker. Whether macho, *joto*, effeminate, or queer, the three are forever icons in the development of biker sexual myth and popular culture.

Third Space Bikers and Police Deployment of Sexuality

Cops didn't care for, or about, such sexually charged, complex icons. Yet, the sexual aspect of biker images seems to have attracted the interests of police personnel from the 1960s through the 1990s. "Third space feminism" relates to a variety of lifestyles for people who are not at one of the two extreme ends of the spectrum that runs between "female" and "male," or "feminine" and "masculine." LGBT people live in all kinds of different third spaces in various places between these two poles. Many members of Raw Thunder, an all-female riding association, tend toward such alternative life orientations. Char Zack, the Road Captain of Raw Thunder, mentions one incident that relates to third space realities and police agency deployment of sexuality. She went to the Laughlin River Run event once—and only once—in the mid-1990s. For like every other motorcyclist that weekend riding on the desert highway that crosses the Colorado River, she was required to go through what bikers call "the gauntlet," a roadblock out in the middle of nowhere consisting of a line of Arizona police gang officers.

All bikes were pulled over, yet cars were exempt and could just drive on by. The regional police power center stood out in the desert heat, drawing overtime pay, waiting for bikers to scrutinize for detention and special treatment. That day, Zack had been riding in an all-male group of riders and was packing another woman on her back seat, a friend who had never been to a run before. As they slowly edged their way through the gauntlet, one officer asked, "So what do we have *here*, a couple of *lesbians?*"

---

[11] Eric Zolov, *Refried Elvis: The Rise of the Mexican Counterculture* (Berkeley: University of California Press, 1999).

This was one of many inappropriate incidents that led to another Foucauldian measure of resistance within the power-structural grid: the routine videotaping, by riders' rights organizations, of police encounters with motorcyclists beginning in the late 1990s. Zack's experience at the river led to a Foucauldian dynamic in which both the gauntlet incident and the biker-organizational response to it are two sides of the same coin, two parts of the same power-knowledge-pleasure system. After all, the intention of the motorcyclists' rights video project is to generate evidence to be used within legal and governmental systems, instruments of the same power structure.

Another reason the gauntlet incident is part of a Foucauldian deployment of sexuality is that it involved detainment of imagined sexually deviant "Others" (both bikers and "lesbian" bikers), state agency naming of imagined rider sexual orientations, and an individual officer getting his psychosexual rocks off through an unprofessional, rude, homophobic comment. Zack vowed never to return to the Laughlin Run. As often happens, police gangs, Harvard psychiatry professors, and other nonriding outsiders to the pleasure of motorcycling lack any real understanding of the ride. They "don't have a clue," as most riders will attest.

Tactical Discourse—Resistance by Bikers and LGBT People

Some bikers appropriate the language used by the power centers. Foucault calls this the "rule of the tactical polyvalence of discourses." Accordingly:

> discourses can be both an instrument and an effect of power, but also . . . a starting point for an opposing strategy. Discourse transmits and produces power; it reinforces it, but also undermines and exposes it, renders it fragile and makes it possible to thwart it. . . . often in the same vocabulary, using the same categories. (pp. 100–01)

Employing such discourse in a resistance within the power structure, some riders would say that, in fact, it is the Harvard doctor, the police agency leadership, and other nonriders like them who are mentally disturbed, frustrated, and jealous to the extent that they have sexual issues with bikers.

Although moto sexuality was a subtle but increasingly significant undercurrent during the twentieth century, gay motorcyclists also emerged with a tactical discourse of their own as early as 1921, when the magazine *Motorcycle and Bicycle Illustrated* published an article. It included the spotlighting of someone who was probably the first lesbian motorcyclist commentator. The anonymous author of the article interviewed several heterosexual women who rode their own bikes, as well as Evelyn Greenway, a West Coast biker who was also a news reporter. Greenway said:

> It makes me disgusted with my sex when I see so many baby dolls lolling back in great clumsy limousines, dependent as a toy poodle on the ability of some "mere man" to get them there and back. For myself, I really pity them. Grace and I enjoy our machines. We both like swimming and fishing and the outdoors generally. We are planning some dandy winter trips. . . . To all red blooded girls I'll say "Do it with a motorcycle." (October 27th, pp. 43–48)

In addition to the moto press, other media productions rubbed against the grain of conventional, straight hetero-normality. For example, in the 1940s Robert Hughes wrote gender-alternative, fictional radio sketches about a female police motor sergeant, inspired by Sappho imagery. These are empowering statements that promote collective liberation, rather than mere defensive stances.

The People, United—Refusing to Obey

Foucault tells us that the accuracy of different biker sexual descriptions is irrelevant. Bikers seem to agree. Foucault would instead call attention to the power centers that build gendered and sexual stereotypes and their strategies. He would ask which companies, corporations, governmental, medical, and other power structures are involved in the construction and perpetuation of labels such as homosexual, sexual outlaw, gender traitor, motorcycle syndrome, lesbians, or mystique. Who benefits from the acceptance of these labels as categories of identity and analysis? Who is it that feels a need to control bikers and queer people? Tactical discourses, rider activists, and others are critical responses to marginalization, within a power structural dynamic, on behalf of everyone that power centers seek to dominate, including LGBT people and riders.

Media, police, and other power centers portray motorcycling as a sexually charged world. Although their images interacted with biker realities for generations—resulting in the alienation and marginalization of both motorcyclists as an imagined sexually deviant social class and of gay, lesbian, and queer bikers—Foucault points out that these definitions are continually contested. He writes, "Confronted by a power that is law, the subject who . . . is 'subjected' . . . is he who obeys" (p. 85).

So, what about those who refuse to obey? Queer voices and the music of Harley engines may help to extend the limits of tolerance as alternative discourses of sexuality continue to engage the interplay between riders, activists, elite authorities, and structures of conformity.[12]

----

[12] I would like to thank Ernesto Chávez and Héctor Carbajal for responding to drafts of this chapter.

14

Riding along the Way: A *Dao* of Riding

DAVID JONES

Soon after arriving, the man took off his watch; he no longer needed to keep time, or so he thought. It would take several days until he realized the depth of his action. Hawai'i made him feel no distinct need for measuring time. His Harley-Davidson Sportser, which he stored with a friend on the North Shore, also made him feel this way. Sporties, as they are affectionately known, are the smallest of Harley's motorcycles, but the quickest and most balanced. This is what interested the man.

He returned to Hawai'i yearly to ride with his friends and escape thinking philosophically. Motorcycles bring their riders into the moment, make them aware of their surroundings and heighten and sharpen the senses. Motorcycles ground their riders to the earth and the earth's flow in natural and human ways like nothing else can. Harley-Davidsons, the most visceral of all bikes, especially bring their riders into an embodied state of awareness. The man needed this yearly experience in order to flee the disembodied state of Western philosophy, which still grappled with its Platonic and Cartesian legacy that seemed to forever place the human species as superior to all others and forever leave it alienated from all that was natural. This legacy conflated soul and mind; it sucked soul out of the body and gave it to spirit; it divided mind and body and pitted thoughts and senses against each other as ways of knowing. The man needed to return to his body, and 550 pounds of Milwaukee's finest pig iron was the perfect prescription for a renewed sense of self. The man would find his soul once again. And caring for the soul was the first definition of philosophy proffered by Plato in his *Apology*.

He sat overlooking the ocean at Ali'i Beach Park in historic Hale'iwa Town. Not consciously realizing, he had deeply inhaled and the smell of the Pacific Ocean filled his nostrils, and after letting go of an unexpected sigh the man felt the first sign of release that he had come to expect in his many visits to these islands over the years. He looked over at his black Sporty, its glistening chrome dual pipes, chrome oil tank, and black textured covers. Silver and black, shiny and dark, smooth and textured—this was his bike. His bike, that brought the polarities together. He had not seen other motorcycles transformed and individualized in this particular way. There was something of him there and in return those humanly constructed gears and what encased them, that rubber, the shiny Harley paint, and his fringed saddle somehow defined him in a significant way. Perhaps it was the strength of his shadow side that brought him to the saddle of this rumbling engine that came to life as he pushed the start button. He didn't quite know for sure exactly, but this thought never entered his mind as he slowly brought the bike to life; and as he rolled on the accelerator, he set it into motion, and he came to life with it.

He rode along the hump of the island between the two volcanic mountain ranges called the Wai'anaes, the older range, and the younger Ko'olaus. These ranges are as distinct as *yin* and *yang*, the receptive and active mutually inclusive principles of Chinese cosmology; the ranges are dry and wet respectively and provide the extremes of the island, and each of the islands with its high rate of endangered plant and animal species and the urban sprawl and its accompanying environmental demands, especially on O'ahu, is a microcosm of the prognosis of the planet. The man knew all of this, but reveled still in what remains one of Earth's Edens. And how better to experience this beauty than on his Harley-Davidson Sporty with the constant throaty mantra of its dual pipes tuned just like any other musical instrument—the sound of which placed the man into a meditative state of awareness and made him feel alive once again and in his body. Over the years of coming to this Eden, the man's bike was slowly transforming into a work of art. Harleys are built to be altered, to become individualized signature events of their riders, and the man was slowly giving his signature to this Harley as it breathed its OM into the early morning chill under the silent gaze of Mt. Ka'ala, the highest point on O'ahu.

As the first chapter of the *Zhuangzi*, that Daoist text so many love, states, he was "Rambling without Destination" this day. Rambling without destination is the Daoist prescription to find the way, the *dao*, to find oneself along the way. He was a sole rider today without his local riding buddies who were attending to the business of making their livings. Even in Hawai'i people need to work. The man enjoyed riding with his friends, especially Ken and Leo who brought him into this world of needing to be attentive and aware of what he was doing, of learning to balance and blend with the forces of sun, wind, water, gravity, and the presence other people who philosopher Jean-Paul Sartre proclaimed could be hell. For motorcycle riders, other people could indeed be hell as they moved about in their compartmentalized realities with climate control, sound systems that make them oblivious to what's around, and their mindless distractions of putting on make-up, eating ice cream and Big Macs, talking on cell phones, and sometimes even reading books, none of which were ever philosophy books that demanded too much attention and focus. Such mindless activities on a motorcycle mean death, and the man came to appreciate the exhilaration of being fully attentive and responsive to the world of which he was invariably a part. To be responsive, he realized, is to be appropriate to the context at hand, which is different from the environmental and ethical view that we are stewards responsible for the environment or for our actions. To ride is to figure out somehow what both the Confucians and Daoists already knew—that each of us needs to respond appropriately to all beings encountered, not to assert ourselves so willingly upon others, but rather to affect a harmony by blending with the flow and learning to affect its flowing when necessary in order to promote meaningful change. Without this meaningful change, life would be random, and perhaps even impossible. The man could see that the presence of so many motorcycles on the streets of O'ahu changed driving patterns; other motorists simply were aware, albeit sometimes only at a remotely subliminal level, that they shared their road space with the two-wheeled. When he had this thought, the man knew this was a good lesson for developing a friendlier way for two-legged humans to live with their four-legged brethren.

Not riding with Ken and Leo this day would place the man in a more Daoist space than a Confucian one where they would spend the day engaged in the practice of *li*, the rites or ritual propriety. When they were together, often times encountering some of the many other riders on Oahu, they would participate in rider *li*. As in any kind of *li*, the objective is to promote well-being and robust, enhanced, and meaningful relationships with others. With these kinds of relationships established, harmony is likely to ensue. One sensed this harmony through the at-first unexpected polite manner in which riders in Hawai'i encounter each other through their communal sense of being on two wheels where life was always held out over death. This was especially and certainly part of the subculture of Harley riders who were even more seemingly polite than their mates who rode atop the non-American bikes from Japan, England, and Italy. All magnificent bikes in their own right, ones that could blow the Harleys off road and track—but nevertheless they simply weren't Harleys. But today, the man was alone. He would circle the island and end where he started, in Hale'iwa Town, the North Shore home to the best surfing in the world, another practice of attuned awareness and balance. The man would be better off for his journey on this day.

The morning was crisp and clear as it often is in Hawai'i. The cool air moved across his face as the sun's rays streamed through the mountains where they intersected with the misting rain of the Ko'olaus and formed a rainbow. The man would see many rainbows this day and would even seek to ride through them, but they would remain evasive, always eluding him as some unreachable horizon. Life itself was this way—there is always that approach to meaning, to love, to intimacy that seems to withdraw at the very last moment and pass over us like the wind moving across the man's face and around his body as he rolled on between the mountains. How to keep our balance through these kinds of experiences is one of our overriding challenges. It too would be his challenge throughout the day.

As he glided to the other side, the man began to feel the warming of the day and the sun's hint of the afternoon. The sun makes Hawai'i the tropical paradise it is, but brutalizes the skin when given a chance. For this rider, sunscreen was more important than wearing a helmet, which inhibited vision, sound, smell, and the feel of the ride no matter what others maintained, no matter what the safety Nazis insisted. If he was going to go down, for sure he wanted full body armor, but to avoid going down was, he often reasoned, even more important. Hawai'i law, despite attempts to change it, allowed riders to expose their heads to wind, sun, rain, and the pavement if fate would have it. The constant attempts to mandate helmet use were well intended, but one can never measure what doesn't happen except by anecdotal evidence and the man had such a story when his full-faced helmet lulled him into a false sense of security, relaxed his head turns, and impaired his hearing and vision. When he almost pulled into the small pickup that day, he immediately pulled over and strapped this piece of gear, which might save his life or prevent some donor recipient from a needed organ some day, to the back of his bike, and there it remained. His unprotected head made him feel freer, and wasn't this what he longed for, wasn't this freedom to go "rambling without destination," without some teleological goal such as Plato's perfect realm, an Abrahamic heaven, or some vision of ultimate reality what he wanted? Wasn't this feeling of being back in his body, to court the death that was always with him anyhow, and simply to be aware of everything around him again—to be alive!—wasn't this what he wanted and why he rode? Wasn't this the reason he came yearly to Hawai'i? And thereafter, this is the way he rode, clad in leather, denim, boots, gloves, and hatless as he made his way, along the way.

He cruised over H1, the only U.S. interstate that never leaves the state, into Waipahu Town, a warmer, drier, and more industrial part of the island. In Waipahu, the man would stop at the Hog Pen, Larry's shop. Larry was the Harley man to whom most riders ultimately found their ways; he was the one who talked the man out of his standard issued pipes and breather and into tweaking his Sporty. Larry was the biker guru, at least for the Harley riders. Like other Harley riders, Larry understood the man's longing for freedom, for rambling without a goal in mind, for riding for the sheer joy of just riding, and understood what it meant to be an accomplished rider, the ruler of one's ride.

But Larry did not consciously know in a scholarly way, as did the man, the trained philosopher, that the accomplished rider is like the *shengren*, the Daoist sagely ruler, who is the rhythmic

expression of the pulsating *dao*, the way, that ebbs and tides as
it gives expression to the *yang* and *yin* of the natural world. The
man's Sporty was this tension of the human-made and the natural, the sounds of the natural and the throaty OM of his cus-
tomed pipes, and it was this tension that brought him into
harmony with the four *qi* of heaven, which are the energetic fluids in the atmosphere and inside the body; these *qi* were in his
body too although often hidden until he sat in the Sporty's saddle. These *qi* are wind and rain, dark and light, and mix with
the five *xing*, the "goings" or processes of wind, fire, soil, metal,
and water that transition reality into a harmonious order in
Chinese philosophy. This is heaven, or *tian*, a heaven on earth
where the sage learns to float in harmony with the apparently
disharmonious transformations of *yin* and *yang*, the four *qi* of
heaven, and the five *xing* of earth that combine to give force to
the changing world; Hawai'i, with its subtlety of change and
power of transformation, is the changing world of *tian* and its
flow. The sage tides and ebbs, lives and dies, with spiritual def-
erence to *dao*'s flow; this is the life the man wished to live.

The man, who was now stripped of any encapsulating structure that dualistically separated his true self—a self of no merit
or fame for the Daoists—became a being without ego as he rode
down the road, along with its flow, with his machine pulsating
under him; it gave him the power to not be his encapsulated
self, to be open to all around him, to be part of the machine
under him, and the pavement under the machine and the earth
under the pavement; it gave him the power, more than just intellectually, to understand Heraclitus's challenge to expect the
unexpected. The man came to expect the unexpected as he
rode westward out of Waipahu down the Wai'anae coast to the
end of the road.

The Wai'anae coast of Oahu is punctuated by the browned
western mountain range of the islands. The Wai'anae Mountains
had been clear-cut for sandalwood and koa trees by early profiteers of Hawai'i's many natural resources. Replanted with euca-
lyptus and other non-native species that flourished in the
tropical sun, the mountain range would be forever transformed.
The volcanic rust brown color of the mountains and their
attending cinder cones that jut out into the remarkably blue
water of the Pacific framed the man's ride as he headed toward
the end of the road. This was the part of the island where many

native Hawaiians were pushed as most of their land was stolen and remains occupied to this day by outside invaders. The man was sensitive to the history and politics and the greed and the self-indulgent gluttony of those who came to these islands and exploited and forever transformed everything in this last of Earth's Edens from its coral reefs to its mountaintops. The ghosts of the first Hawaiians, those Polynesians who sailed the great expanse of ocean to these most remote islands on the planet, do not even recognize most of the plants they encounter on their nightly spirit walks in search of their original early paradise. As the man rode along the hot stretch of coastal road protected only by his denim jacket, pants, boots, gloves, sunglasses, and sunscreen, young girls and boys would smile and wave when their parents weren't looking. Harleys were the bike of choice on the Wai'anae Coast, and this sentiment brought a smile to the man's face and a feeling of connection in his heart.

As he approached the end of the road another rider streaked passed him on a red Kawasaki or Suzuki; its whining engine sound reminded the man of rapidly flapping insect wings that sounded distant and got louder as the insect approached. And approach he did, and with incredible speed. The man reacted to seeing the rider approach as he did with all other riders on Oahu by giving the man the low greeting of an extended hand, biker *li* in Hawai'i, but the helmeted rider was focused on just the road before him. With no more of his throttle remaining, he streaked passed the Sporty; it was an awesomely fast bike. The man himself once approached the century mark of 100 m.p.h. one night on an open road and understood the thrill of speed, but on this day he was cruising. At the end of the road, he stopped at the beach park and took a prolonged moment with the sparkling ocean and the sound of the ocean's rhythmic approach to the shore. He filled his lungs with the smell of ocean and wondered if the specters of Hawai'i past could still smell its familiar fragrance. This, he thought, was the one thing that could never be destroyed for them. The man stayed until a thumping stereo of someone enjoying the beach in a much different way interrupted his meditation. Riding along the way back, not far from where he was passed by the intent rider, he saw the flashing lights of the ambulance and the police cars and the mangled, misshapen red bike off to the side of the road. The man knew the young man to be dead; there was no way anyone could survive at that speed. Over a beer and lunch in Wai'anae, he honored the unknown rider, who was, he hoped, an organ donor. Giving life, being a part of another, was the Daoist thing to do. This day was the young biker's, not his.

There is only one way in and out of Wai'anae unless one has an off-road vehicle. Retracing his way, the man decided to head for the coolness of the Windward Side where the chance of getting wet was almost predictable. Bypassing historic Hale'iwa Town, the man headed down the North Shore where the Ko'olau Mountains collected clouds and dumped rain, usually in the form of passing showers. This side of the island is wetter, greener, and windy. With the blue ocean and its turquoise waters around the coral reefs and the light brown sand to his left and the rippling green spine like mountains to his right, the man leisurely rode the coast where fragrant smells from passing flowers wafted their ways to his nostrils. Waiting out the rain is always a good idea for once wet coldness invariably sets in even under the warm riding conditions in Hawai'i. But sometimes one just can't escape the forces of nature and the man got wet; his shiny bike got spotted with watermarks and dirt from the road. He accepted the rain and the coldness that followed as he made his way along H3, the most expensive and one of the most beautiful stretches of Interstate in the country. H3, a main artery along with the Pali Highway and the Likelike Highway, connects the Windward and Leeward sides and flows into various spots of the city side of the island when traveling across the mountains to the town side of Honolulu. Here he rolled on his throttle and felt his Sporty come to life, the patented "potato-potato-potato" sound of the engine transformed into its throaty OM chant of his custom pipes that never once paused for a breath. The change of speed heightened the man's senses a notch as he achieved perfect poise on the massively vibrating human-made machine whose power can provoke the foolishness of a ruling ego as its seductive rumbling affirms and enlivens form and power. But his ego wasn't foolish; he had left that behind somewhere when he exhaled at the beginning of the day at Ali'i Beach Park. He felt the flowing currents of *qi* through his body and the presence of the zone as he entered its nearness.

Accomplished riders, like Cook Ding in the *Zhuangzi*, who never sharpens his cleaver as he cuts through ligament, carti-

lage, muscle, but never hits the bone, learn the art of the ride
and appropriate what the Daoists call *wuwei*. *Wuwei* is a spontaneous yet learned skill that arises as a naturally emergent
action perfectly appropriate to the context of encountered situations that can change suddenly and dramatically. *Wuwei* literally means no-action, but the Daoist sensibility is to act as if not
acting, to leave the ego behind and just perform one's actions
naturally and harmoniously within the situation at hand—the
dancer is the dance, the lover the loving, and the rider the riding. The sagely rider who overcomes this seduction of the controlling ego's will by his mastery on the road shapes the
structure, focuses the energy of the road's flow, and performs
actions so perfectly, skillfully, and appropriately that he appears
to do so without effort—the way of *dao* is *wuwei*. A sagely rider
is fluid and melds with the system of the bike, the road, and the
transformations of *yin* and *yang*, the four *qi*, and the five *xing*
of the earth. As the earth moves, the conditions of the road
move, and as the road moves so does the rider. The man was
balanced at his high speed, and leaning into his turns with the
pitch of the road, he was poised for anything. The rush of the
leaning into turns came and passed without attachment. He felt
as though he were in the heart of the system, conjoined with its
forces, and it was through his training on this 550 pound vibrating human-made machine that he was adept at being a part of
his world—all of this without the presence of thought. Coming
into town he realized he had appropriated the *qi* at will and that
dao had flowed through him and that this stretch of open road
flowed through him as if the arteries of the earth gave him the
power, the *de*, of *wuwei*, which flowed through all things. He
felt as though he had made his way home.

The *yang* of the day was moving toward its *yin*. The man
always enjoyed a brief run through Waikiki along Kalakaua
where he was greeted by the smell of coconut tanning oil, burnt
bodies of tourists from around the world, and the sight of
Diamond Head jutting out with splendor into the Pacific. He
couldn't stay long around so many people with their many vaca-
tion demands, but this too was important for him to occasion-
ally experience because it reminded him how he had his own
set of demands for coming. He headed out the Lunalilo Freeway
toward the North Shore where he would park his Sporty and
hook up with friends for food, drink, and conversation. "Talking

story," as it is referred to in Hawai'i, is a vital part of life. He too would have his stories about the fallen rider, hitting the zone over the Ko'olaus, and the smiling children on the Wai'anae Coast.

His route home took him close to Pearl City where he remembered a former student who emigrated from Vietnam and had opened an Italian restaurant some years back. He wondered if the hardworking student had made it and was delighted to see the restaurant's proprietor greet him with a warm smile of *aloha*. And it was from there he set out down the busy street with its ebbing flow of traffic, thumping stereos, and many intersections; from the restaurant he set out for the hump between the mountain ranges toward the North Shore, for all journeys on an island, the microcosm of this planet, end where they begin.

Kamehameha Highway was busy toward the end of the day with the after-work crowd who waited out rush hour before heading to their homes in Pearl City, Mililani, and Wahiawa. Some were heading for Kapolei, a new planned city to handle O'ahu's urban sprawl. The man rode his Harley through the remnants of the day's "tropical traffic." The traffic wasn't quite stop and go; it moved with an irregular flow—not quite stop and go, but not freely open either. Every time he managed to get his bike into either third or fourth gear, this main artery homeward for so many would get clogged, or all "choked" as his buddy Leo would say. He was tired, it had been a long day, and there were dinner plans for later that evening. But he was in no hurry. The sun was ready to dip behind the horizon. Locals and tourists alike would gather for the day's main event—the setting of the sun and the birth of the rising moon. Hawai'i made the man realize what Heraclitus meant when he said the "sun was new every day." The man always tried to watch the spectacular sunsets when he was in Hawai'i, but this day he would just bask in its afterglow. Finally, the traffic seemed to break and that wonderful feeling of moving freely brought relief and air to his lungs. His Sporty rumbled beneath him as he moved through the gears—second, third, fourth—and just as he was ready to hit fifth the traffic immediately choked in front of him. The setting sun pierced through his sunglasses and he momentarily missed the red suggestion of the brake lights in front of him. His left toe brought the smallest but the quickest and most balanced of Harley's motorcycles into fifth-gear position and he let out the clutch and the Sporty responded like a horse wanting the barn. Finally, some air! Finally some freedom!

It was then, at that moment of freedom, the exhilaration of the promise of open road, that the man saw the dotted sea of red in front of him; it was then he saw the quickly approaching container truck stopped in front of him; it was then he remembered the young biker of the morning; and it was then he responded. The man applied the clutch, down shifted, firmly squeezed the hand lever that controlled the front brake, and pressed down on the foot brake pedal that controlled the rear wheel all in a singular motion, so choreographed that only the most disciplined eye would have been able to discern the unison of the individual executions. He heard the voice in his head, "You never want to high-side your motorcycle. You never want to release your rear brake once it's locked and skidding." The back wheel locked, which meant he was losing traction, and that meant control; the transmission grumbled as it experienced the unexpected lower gear, and the tail end of the bike began to skid from side to side under the friction of the rear tire's rubber of the locked wheel. He backed off the brake just a bit to gain more traction, but heard the voice of his teacher in his head again, "You never want to high-side your motorcycle. You never want to release your rear brake once it's locked and skidding." To fight the natural tendency to grab, not squeeze, and only use the front brake, which is much more efficient but in this situation when used alone could send the rider over the bars, requires discipline, and there is never freedom without discipline. But the front wheel chirped. "You don't want to lock the front brake," the voice in his head seemed to say clearly. The man trusted this voice of Morgan, his instructor. "She'll be so upset with me," he thought, "for not wearing my helmet and dying on the high side." Only the discerning eye of an adept rider could understand the beauty of controlling a front and rear wheel skid almost simultaneously.

The man released the front brake for a split second, then immediately reapplied it, squeezing, not grabbing, and the front wheel gained traction with the earth under it and unlocked. The bike shimmied with its rider poised on top of it, he held his knees tightly against the black shiny gas tank, and he kept his head up with his eyes looking ahead with the front wheel straight. Any change in his path while stopping would surely high-side him in the opposite direction over his motorcycle, and he knew this would likely kill him; riders just don't survive this kind of fall. He needed to keep the front wheel straight until he came to a complete stop. But there just wasn't enough room for the motorcycle to stop. The message became boldly visible: "WARNING, THIS TRUCK MAKES FREQUENT STOPS!" Collision was inevitable. And it was at this moment of realization the man jettisoned his individualized signature black Sporty, with its shiny chrome dual pipes, chrome oil tank, and black textured covers—he would be taking the low-side. Out of the corner of his eye he would later remember the sparks generated from metal meeting pavement, the gasping sound of the Sporty's stalling breath, and the smell of the Sporty's bodily fluids. But his focus was on the approaching rear guard of the truck and its message of warning that this truck makes frequent stops. He was sliding on his buttocks with his left leg somewhat tucked under the right and with his left arm slowing his momentum as much as he could. He held his head up with his right arm wrapped around and his hand grasping the back of his neck. Curiously he felt no pain, but somehow realized his head was positioned in line with the low guard in front of him. Lowering his head at the last moment, the man continued his slide as if into home plate, and gradually came to rest under the rear axle of the truck.

The man felt himself breathing as he looked up at the underside of the truck; he contemplated the huge universal joint looking back at him with its unblinking studded third eye in its middle. Its silent gaze punctuated the closeness of life and death and the universe's utter indifference toward any particular member of any species. From this perspective, he realized he was dispensable. All meaning is created. And Beyond, Mt. Ka'ala gazed down upon the scene from above the clouds that shrouded its indifferent expression. The man methodically inventoried his body. He could move, and he felt the great need to move out from under the belly of the massive monster that swallowed him. The man emerged and slowly got to his feet. He noticed the red-orange glow of the sky, felt the trade winds welcoming him back to life, and stood on the firmness of what was the wake of motion just a moment ago.

The man felt as though he were still moving, but now it felt as though he were sliding through an empty space; this feeling of sliding through the cold darkness of empty space would be forever with him thereafter. Later, the gaze of the universe's indifference would accompany him through this empty space— all meaning is created—and he would come to realize he projected this gaze; there was, after all, no gaze, just indifference except for the people who gathered around with their concerned faces and looks of astonished shock as they beheld this man in ragged leathers and denims in front of them. How was he alive, he imagined. Why was he not hurt? Later the soreness would find its way from his body's depths and a fractured hand would make itself present, but the road rash would somehow be minimal. He called Larry from the hospital where he was released after being checked over and they picked up his mangled motorcycle. Larry drove him to the North Shore where he met up with Leo and Ken for their late dinner. "Hey man, keep 'em up next time." All the man could do was smile at Larry as he closed the door. Over dinner, the man told the stories of the day, of how he got into the zone over the Koʻolaus, drove through a rainbow, and of the high-pitched sound of death passing without any acknowledgment to him from the young rider in Waiʻanae. They drank a toast to the dead rider. It was, after all, his day.

The man told his friends that his bike would be in the shop for a while, and that he would be joining the ranks of the four-wheeled, compartmentalized majority until his bike got a once-over—some cosmetic surgery he told them. The man excused himself, explaining it had been a long day, and slowly walked toward home for the pain was beginning to find its way to him; the drugs were wearing off. That day, he made the remainder of his way on foot. He remembered the *Zhuangzi*, "The way is made by walking it." He smiled, and then found himself smiling broadly for his life, and the life of the dead rider, for he had spent the entire day blending with and emerging from the unfolding and pulsating road of *Dao*.

Contributors' Dream Machines

STEVEN E. ALFORD teaches at Nova Southeastern University in Fort Lauderdale, Florida. He has dithered frequently in print about Paul Auster, is currently shepherding *Two Wheels to Freedom: Discovering Motorcycle Culture* (edited along with Gary Kieffner and Susan Buck) into fame and publication fortune, and is on the board of the one and only online, refereed motorcycle journal (ijms.nova.edu). In the occasional absence of hurricane-force winds but always in sauna-like temperatures, he rides a Honda VTX 1800C and a Triumph Sprint ST (but not at the same time).

RANDALL E. AUXIER went over the handlebars of his Honda XL-70 at age fourteen while jumping a hill in the river bottoms near Memphis, and learned the hard way (the only way he learns anything) to pull up on the handlebars when taking a jump at thirty-five m.p.h. He also learned how much an XL-70 weighs in Earth gravity when multiplied by thirty-two feet per second squared, times twenty feet, leading him to an interest in physics. While being removed from the area on the back of Tommy Arendale's Kawasaki 175, he was conceiving of his essays for this volume, clutching his cracked ribs, and silently thanking God he had never read Bernie Rollins's essay on helmet laws. Because of this gap in his reading, he lived to teach philosophy at Southern Illinois University, Carbondale.

CRAIG BOURNE has been a philosopher at the University of Cambridge for far too long. Realizing this, he decided at twenty-three to have a premature mid-life crisis, developed a fetish for Italian motorcycles, and can often found wandering the streets in tight colorful leathers. When he isn't risking life and limb on a Ducati, he likes to throw himself from planes. He hopes one day to be able to combine these two activities in the greatest stunt the world has ever seen. But when he's not daydreaming, he likes to play the guitar and the drums. Although his neighbors are not too convinced about his evident musical genius, they are often very encouraging about his genuine potential as a stuntman (see above). To find out more and to read some of his work in metaphysics, logic and the philosophy of science, visit http://cpb .blueorange.net, which can also be found by following links from his page on the Cambridge University Philosophy Faculty website at http://www.phil.cam.ac.uk.

FRED FELDMAN is a professor of philosophy at the University of Massachusetts at Amherst, where he has been on the faculty since 1969. He is the author of *Pleasure and the Good Life: On the Nature, Varieties, and Plausibility of Hedonism* (2004), *Utilitarianism, Hedonism, and Desert* (1997), *Confrontations with the Reaper: A Philosophical Study of the Nature and Value of Death* (1992), *Doing the Best We Can: An Essay in Informal Deontic Logic* (1986), and several other books and more than seventy papers in professional journals such as *The Philosophical Review, The Journal of Philosophy, Mind, Analysis, Noûs, Philosophical Studies,* and *Philosophy and Phenomenological Research.* He is perhaps best known for his work in connection with the Bard College Motorcycle Club, where he was a founding co-president in 1961. He's also known to the Providence, Rhode Island, Fire Department for his participation in a minor conflagration involving a motorcycle in his living room in 1967. He wishes to assure everyone that he no longer runs his motorcycles in his home.

SUZANNE FERRISS is a professor of English at Nova Southeastern University in Fort Lauderdale, Florida, a sprawling urban wasteland with few twisties but a year-round riding season. Her publications include two volumes on the cultural study of fashion—*On Fashion* and *Footnotes: On Shoes*—as well as *A Handbook of Literary Feminisms* and *Chick Lit: The New Woman's Fiction.* She also helps manage the *International Journal of Motorcycle Studies* (ijms.nova.edu). When riding her 2005 Yamaha FZ1—in Liquid Silver, the fastest color—she wears a protective mesh jacket, boots with stylishly functional platform heels, and a full-face helmet that exactly matches her bike.

JON GOLDSTEIN is professor of economics at Bowdoin College located in Brunswick on the Maine coast. He has published studies on the effectiveness of motorcycle helmets. In the 1980s, he testified in six state legislatures against helmet law legislation and was active in Maine's bikers' rights movement. He has ridden motorcycles since 1969 and currently owns a 1958 Harley-Davidson FLH, a 1973 Norton 750 Combat Commando, and a 1986 BMW R80. Once he led a group of fifty hard-core Harley riders through Freeport, Maine (famous for the outdoor retailer L.L. Bean) destined for a biker event. Upon coming across a busload of disembarking tourists, he pulled the procession over to ask for directions to L.L. Bean and received the expected incredulous stares from the tourist citizenry.

CAROLYN M. GRAY was the assistant to the VP of Marketing for Eaglemark, a subsidiary of Harley-Davidson Financial Services, from 1998–1999. During this time she experienced her first Daytona Bike Week, and since then has been in training to become the next cole slaw wrestling champion. She should be ready for her first match in 2008. Carolyn also has a B.A. in creative writing from Columbia College, Chicago, and completed the Gonsoulin Labor Leadership Program for union organizers at DePaul University.

GRAHAM HARMAN is Assistant Professor of Philosophy at the American University in Cairo, Egypt. He sometimes bears an uncanny resemblance to the Peter Fonda character in *Easy Rider*. He is also the author of three books: *Tool-Being* (2002), *Guerrilla Metaphysics* (2005), and *Heidegger Explained* (forthcoming).

DAVID JONES teaches philosophy somewhere in Georgia. There's speculation he may be teaching at some elite institution, but in reality he probably teaches at some nondescript state school such as Kennesaw State University. This much we seem to know: his publications are mostly in the areas of Chinese and Greek philosophy. Inside sources have it that his current book project, *The Fractal Self: Intimacy and Emergence in the Universe* is with the Hawai`i based biologist John L. Culliney. Reports indicate the book is a cross-fertilization study between complex biological systems and ancient Greek, Daoist, Confucian, and Buddhist approaches to self-nature relationships. In addition, it is believed he has edited four books, with one forthcoming from Open Court (*Contemporary Encounters with Confucius*). His work appears in an array of journals and book chapters that have such bizarre titles as "Toward an Ecology of Compassion: *Homo Specialis*, Animality, and Buddha-Nature," "Ecological Self-so-ing in the *Liezi*," and "The Empty Soul: Nietzsche, Nishitani, and the Good" they're probably made up! Although perhaps as apocryphal, he's the founding editor of *East-West Connections* and allegedly was the East-West Center's 2004 *Most Distinguished Alumnus*. Although no one remembers having seen or spoken to him, he received his Ph.D. in Comparative Philosophy from the University of Hawai`i. There have been, however, occasional sightings of someone looking like the man in his account bathed in the shadowy light of a Hawai'i moon riding a Sportster with throaty chrome pipes and an incandescent Harley Davidjones on its black tank.

GARY L. KIEFFNER is a doctoral student in the Borderlands History Ph.D. Program, University of Texas at El Paso, where he also teaches U.S. history. He serves on the editorial board of the International Journal of Motorcycle Studies, available online at www.ijms.nova.edu.

Kieffner has actively participated in the motorcycling community through riders' civil rights organizations for many years and has ridden on the open road forever. He rode his current two-wheeler, a 1992 Harley-Davidson XL, for 169,000 miles before completing the construction of a Volkswagen trike—a five-year project—in 2004. All of his friends are named after animals, anatomical parts, or inanimate tools.

KERRI MOMMER, Ph.D., (linguistics, Northwestern), is a philosophy book editor in Chicago. Her bike is a pure blue Schwinn. A favorite destination is the Black Hills of South Dakota because she finds that in the shadows of the Ponderosa pines and under the gaze of Crazy Horse, it all becomes clear.

CYNTHIA PINEO is a book editor who enjoys web design and convincing people to write scholarly essays on odd topics. After reading Randy Auxier's chapter about coffee houses and biker bars, she realized that her dream machine is Cowboy's vintage 49E Hydra-Glide, 61ci, V-twin, medium compression, four-speed, restored to the original peacock blue. She might restore it to Kool-Aid purple instead of peacock blue, but that's probably her unfortunate coffeehouse aesthetic talking.

ALAN R. PRATT is a Professor of Humanities at Embry-Riddle Aeronautical University in Daytona Beach, Florida. He writes about nihilism as well as motorcycle culture. *Black Humor: Critical Essays*, *The Critical Response to Andy Warhol*, and *The Dark Side: Thoughts on the Futility of Life* reflect his interest in Nothing. As a nod to Florida's new, relaxed handlebar law, he recently added eighteen-inch ape hangers to his ride. "It's impractical and uncomfortable," he reports," but there's a price to be paid to be cool."

GRAHAM PRIEST is Boyce Gibson Professor of Philosophy at the University of Melbourne. Australia is a great place to ride a bike. He is also Arché Professorial Fellow at the University of St. Andrews. Scotland is not a good place to ride a bike—unless you are a masochist. He has written lots of papers on logic, and other areas ranging from the foundations of quantum mechanics to sexual perversion. He has also written a number of books, including *Beyond the Limits of Thought*. Many of his friends tell him that riding a motor bike is beyond the limits of thought. (Shows little imagination.) When not doing philosophy or bike riding (not incompatible activities), he enjoys practicing karate-do, and wondering what on earth that has to do with Zen.

BERNARD E. ROLLIN is University Distinguished Professor of Philosophy, Professor of Biomedical Sciences, and Professor of Animal Sciences at Colorado State University. He acquired his first motorcycle at age eighteen, and has since logged a quarter of a million motorcycle miles, 90,000 on his current Harley, a 1986 low-rider, or FXRS to the cognoscenti. His son, however, has been riding since age four, when Rollin obsessively forced him to drive a cycle with training wheels. Rollin is the author of fourteen books, the latest of which is *Science and Ethics*, published by Cambridge University Press, over 300 articles, and has given over a thousand invited lectures in twenty-eight countries. A weight-lifter, he has bench-pressed over five hundred pounds.

Hardcore Index